NATIONAL DEFENSE RESEARCH INSTITUTE

T0288555

Assessing Continuous Evaluation Approaches for Insider Threats

How Can the Security Posture of the U.S. Departments and Agencies Be Improved?

David Luckey, David Stebbins, Rebeca Orrie, Erin Rebhan, Sunny D. Bhatt, Sina Beaghley

Prepared for the Office of the Secretary of Defense

For more information on this publication, visit www.rand.org/t/RR2684

Library of Congress Cataloging-in-Publication Data is available for this publication.
ISBN: 978-1-9774-0194-6

Published by the RAND Corporation, Santa Monica, Calif.
© Copyright 2019 RAND Corporation
RAND® is a registered trademark.

Cover: Photo by Andrea Danti / stock.adobe.com.

Support RAND
Make a tax-deductible charitable contribution at
www.rand.org/giving/contribute

www.rand.org

Preface

This exploratory project examines various continuous evaluation (CE) approaches to detecting insider threats that are available to the U.S. government and assesses the relevance of these approaches to the challenges posed by such insider threats. Our report defines CE as a vetting and adjudication process to review on an ongoing basis the background of an individual who has been determined eligible for access to classified information or to hold a sensitive position at any time during the period of eligibility. There are potential benefits from CE in effectiveness and cost over the current method of granting security clearances to personnel based on periodic reinvestigation and readjudication. CE, however, has yet to be widely adopted. Over the previous decade, trusted insiders have caused extreme harm to the United States and its citizens. The scope of threats of future attacks by those who have been deemed trustworthy could range from modest to catastrophic. What capabilities exist to combat insider threats? What aspects of CE are being implemented to address insider threats? What are some costs and benefits of CE? What could be considered in the future? In this report, we will explore these and other questions.

This report should be of interest to the U.S. Department of Defense, the U.S. Intelligence Community, and all other public and private organizations with cleared populations or that face a higher risk of threat from insiders. This research was sponsored by the Office of the Secretary of Defense and conducted within the Cyber and Intelligence Policy Center of the RAND National Defense Research Institute (NDRI), a federally funded research and development center (FFRDC) sponsored by the Office of the Secretary of Defense, the Joint Staff, the Unified Combatant Commands, the Navy, the Marine Corps, the defense agencies, and the Intelligence Community. For more information on the Cyber and Intelligence Policy Center, see www.rand.org/nsrd/ndri/centers/intel or contact the director (contact information is provided on the webpage).

Contents

Figures and Tables

Figures

Tables

Summary

The threat from insiders is not new; the fact that there are costs due to national security and intelligence leaks have been known since the founding of the United States, and the tragedy of physical violence that has been conducted by coworkers is nearly incomprehensible. Over the past decade in particular, trusted U.S. government insiders have murdered fellow workers and physically and psychologically injured others. Insiders have also caused what some government experts have estimated as billions of dollars and irreparable damage to the United States through the unauthorized disclosure of national security information.[1] U.S. alliances have been negatively affected, domestic and international trust in U.S. institutions has been reduced, and some current and potential federal employees have lost confidence in the ability of the very government they serve to provide for their security.[2]

The trustworthiness of those who guard the secrets of the United States should be beyond reproach. The United States needs a process and systems that can assess trustworthiness as required. The current security clearance process is based on periodic and aperiodic investigations and adjudication, and this process and the systems that support it are decades old. Technology has advanced significantly since this system was put in place; an updated, improved system and process could capitalize on these technological advancements. The threat from insiders is very real, and this insider threat puts the United States and U.S. government employees at risk. U.S. department and agency data and the physical security of personnel employed by the United States and those who conduct business at or visit U.S. facilities are at risk from this threat. The costs due to the erosion of confidence by U.S. employees, the U.S. population, and U.S. allies are also significant. While all the direct costs of continuous evaluation (CE)

---

[1] See, for example, Mark Memmott and Eyder Peralta, "Attack at the Navy Yard: Gunman and 12 Victims Killed," NPR, September 16, 2013; Tony Capra, "Snowden Leaks Could Cost Military Billions: Pentagon," NBC News, March 6, 2017; and Carlo Muñoz, "Brennan: Intel Leaks Have 'Absolutely' Damaged US National Security," *The Hill*, August 11, 2012.

[2] See, for example, Katie Connolly, "Has Release of Wikileaks Documents Cost Lives?" BBC News, December 1, 2010.

are not known, comparisons of estimates with current processes could reveal potential savings over time.

Definitions for *insider threat* and *CE* vary among industries and will likely continue to evolve. For this report, we define *insider threat* as "the potential for an individual who has or had authorized access to an organization's assets to use their access, either maliciously or unintentionally, to act in a way that could negatively affect the organization or national security."[3] We define *CE* as "a vetting process to review the background of an individual who has been determined to be eligible for access to classified information or to hold a sensitive position at any time during the period of eligibility."[4]

The threat from insiders is likely to increase in the near term.[5] There will be more incidents in the future, causing harm to both U.S. data and employees. The U.S. government should employ the most thorough form of vetting available to mitigate the threat to the extent possible. Neglecting to do so is potentially irresponsible and dangerous, as demonstrated by the many cases of harm caused by insiders.

One solution that some have advocated is employing a CE process whereby individuals are reviewed in near-real time. This could potentially improve vetting of the trusted workforce and possibly also reduce the actual costs associated with the security clearance and suitability/fitness vetting processes. Despite concerns by some over protection of personal privacy, it is possible that CE may prove less invasive than current investigative approaches for the cleared population. The substance of the data that a CE program would review is not wholly different from data reviewed in the current process. What would change is the frequency with which the data are reviewed and analyzed. The individuals receiving greater scrutiny could be limited to those whom the CE system identified as potentially having an issue worthy of further investigation instead of reviewing random groups of individuals or the entire cleared population, as is currently the case.

While the U.S. government has thought about insider threats for decades, threats such as Chelsea Manning and Edward Snowden (trusted insiders who stole and released classified data) and U.S. Army Major Nidal Hasan (who killed 13 and injured more than 30 at Fort Hood, Texas) have provided momentum to make attempts at resolution. The proliferation of more advanced methods allows for creation of a system that

---

[3]   Modified from a definition seen at Daniel Costa, "CERT Definition of 'Insider Threat'—Updated," *Insider Threat Blog*, Carnegie Mellon University Software Engineering Institute, March 7, 2017, and RAND Corporation, "Security Mandatory Annual Refresher Training (SMART) 2016 Security Training Presentation," undated.

[4]   Executive Order 13764, "Amending the Civil Service Rules, Executive Order 13488, and Executive Order 13467 to Modernize the Executive Branch-Wide Governance Structure and Processes for Security Clearances, Suitability and Fitness for Employment, and Credentialing, and Related Matters," *Federal Register*, Vol. 82, No. 13, January 23, 2017, pp. 8115–8129.

[5]   See, for example, Aaron Boyd, "Manning/Snowden Leaks: The Threat from Within Emerges," *Federal Times*, December 4, 2015.

goes beyond categorizing insider threats from a binary distinction—a threat or not a threat—to a more flexible and comprehensive method categorized by intent, which accounts for variants in the degree and type of access an insider holds, as well as the scope and nature of physical, fiscal, and informational harm that a threat can pose.

The existing literature suggests that despite differences between the various industries involved in CE efforts, the best practices for the CE of insider threats are common across industries. These include conducting risk assessments, fostering a work culture of security awareness, building a threat monitoring system based on conducted risk assessments, and building robust security policies and infrastructure. In areas where current practices need improvement, the challenges to enhancing CE are also common across industries. While behavioral components of an insider threat program may strengthen monitoring, most behavioral approaches suffer from the same challenge of limited to no baseline data. Additionally, technological approaches already play a substantial role in efforts to mitigate insider threats, but they cannot prevent, detect, or weaken insider threats alone.

Many CE programs, particularly within the government, remain in the early phases and are not yet fully operational. The effectiveness of these programs remains somewhat obscure, as most results are not yet publicly available, and it could take time to realize measurable benefits and assess success. The efficiency of CE compared with current methods, however, suggests that CE could offer a less costly alternative in the long run. This does not imply that CE presents a flawless solution to all insider threat problems, as novel issues will likely accompany CE. Privacy concerns, security of data, and alternate potential uses of CE information, as well as issues that have not yet been considered, will have to be explored. Furthermore, CE does not imply a complete replacement of the current system but could serve to improve it. Many challenges lie ahead in developing CE as a solution to insider threats.

As a way of approaching these issues, the research team conducted this exploratory study to examine various methods and metrics for evaluating CE approaches available to the U.S. government and assess the relevance of these approaches to the insider threat challenges faced by national security agencies and departments of the U.S. government. While all aspects of CE implementation are not yet known, the study team was able to conclude that there are some identifiable potential benefits. In this report, we explored questions such as: What capabilities exist to combat insider threat? What aspects of CE are being implemented to address insider threats? What are some costs and benefits of CE? What should be considered in the future? After consideration of these questions, the report identifies several findings regarding insider threat and CE approaches and policy and then offers recommendations for policymakers in federal departments and agencies to consider.

Methodology

The United States currently employs an investigative and adjudicative security clearance process with origins in the Second World War. Technology and knowledge about human behavior have improved dramatically since the creation of this process. RAND researchers sought to assess the efficiency and effectiveness of CE through the review of documents and literature on insider threats and CE and interviews with experts from areas involved in ongoing efforts to improve the process. The authors reviewed the literature on various CE approaches, considered CE cost estimates, examined efficacy and best practices, and assessed some of the practicalities of employing CE. The goal of this report is to assess CE approaches in hopes of informing leaders in the U.S. Department of Defense (DoD), the U.S. Intelligence Community (IC), and other federal government departments and agencies as they consider insider threats and whether to replace or augment the current security clearance investigation and adjudication process.

Findings and Recommendations

In this report, the study team highlights ten findings regarding CE and insider threats and offers recommendations pertinent to those findings for policymakers in federal departments and agencies to consider:

- **Finding 1: There is no commonly shared definition of *insider threat* across the government.** The federal government has focused its definition of *insider threat* almost entirely on foreign adversaries and counterintelligence. The private-sector information technology (IT) and cyber definitions focus on theft of intellectual property and financial assets and harm to organizational systems. Academia expands from the government and private sector to further define and model potential insider threats. These definitions highlight that the actual insider threat may have *already left* the organization.
- **Recommendation 1: Establish a common definition of *insider threat* to facilitate intragovernmental efforts, such as "the potential for an individual who has or had authorized access to an organization's assets to use their access, either maliciously or unintentionally, to act in a way that could negatively affect the organization or national security."** Because insiders have used their trusted access to the workplace to injure and kill employees and others, the definition should clarify that insider threats include those wishing to cause physical harm to employees and visitors to the workplace. This could include both intent and negligence among the terms that determine an insider's capacity to threaten, injure, kill, or harm employees and to undermine national security interests and infrastructure.

- **Finding 2: Neither *CE* nor *insider threat* has been defined in statute.** Although commonalties exist, attempts to define both CE and insider threat across the defense, intelligence, and private sectors vary. A 2015 Government Accountability Office report found that the service components needed a policy that addresses CE.

- **Recommendation 2: Establish a common definition of *CE*, such as "a vetting and adjudication process to review on an ongoing basis the background of an individual who has been determined eligible for access to classified information or to hold a sensitive position at any time during the period of eligibility."** As with most definitions, it is important that the definition of CE is consistent with its application. There are likely benefits to having a common definition of insider threat and CE programs across the public and private sectors. Any future developments in the definition or application of CE should also extend to both the public and private sectors.

- **Finding 3: While the U.S. government has thought about insider threats for many years, threats over the past decade, such as Manning, Snowden, and Hasan, have provided momentum in attempts at resolving those threats.** These cases and others led to categorizing insider threats by intent as opposed to considering them exclusively on a binary scale as threats or not threats.

- **Recommendation 3: Because insider threats exist across a broad spectrum, it would be useful to categorize insider threats in attempting to reduce and mitigate them.** Intent is often an explicit threat indicator among insider categories; by contrast, negligence is not. While negligence does not necessarily imply intent, negligence, as committed by insiders who fall under the *well-intentioned* category of insider (i.e., someone who commits violations through ignorance), for example, should also be considered a threat because it introduces serious liability and consequences.

- **Finding 4: There are limited behavioral or technical data available to develop and deploy an effective and predictive CE monitoring tool.** Scholars and practitioners of CE have been forced to develop technical solutions based on generalized behavioral indicators because access to actual insider threats and their associated data streams is not available. Without ground-truth data on past incidents and behaviors, effective anomaly detection can only be modeled. There have been some attempts to marry behavioral and technological CE efforts within the U.S. IC, but limitations, such as receiving too many false alarms, coupled with a lack of risk indicators to feed IT detections systems provide little value in mitigating actual threats.

- **Recommendation 4: Conduct a thorough academic and scientific review of behavioral approaches predicting insider threat behavior before it occurs.**

The federal government, private sector, and academic community should work together to develop an effective way to share the unique data and behavioral traits gained from actual insider cases. Where access is limited about the actual insiders, investigative field notes and interrogation reports may provide the descriptors necessary to build a more effective program.

- **Finding 5: Public- and private-sector organizations have experienced an increase in the number of insider threat incidents in the period surrounding an employee's termination.** The 30-day period both before and after an employee has left an organization is critical and requires increased focus for CE programs. There are notable instances of insiders looking to cause damage in the event of nonvoluntary separation and other instances in which employees have taken organizational intellectual property to bring to their next job.
- **Recommendation 5: Increase the frequency of continuous monitoring efforts surrounding the period of an employee's termination in both public- and private-sector CE programs.** Continuous monitoring programs, by their nature, will occur more frequently than currently established Office of Personnel Management (OPM) and other agency security clearance readjudication processes. However, future CE implementation should ensure that this frequency is increased in termination situations. In addition, there may be other similar instances (e.g., notable life changes, negative coworker reports or evaluations) in which the frequency of CE must be increased.

- **Finding 6: There is no centralized or authorized facility to receive anonymous reporting streams for individuals in either cleared or uncleared populations.** We noted the lack of a formalized reporting mechanism that could be used to supplement CE processes. For example, family members, coworkers, or neighbors might be aware of or witness individual events that many times go unreported during the standard security, suitability, and fitness processes.
- **Recommendation 6: Create a real-time reporting mechanism to supplement any future security clearance approach, including one involving CE.** This might assist in preventing the next Fort Hood shooting, WikiLeaks upload, or insider-espionage ring. Who should close family members or neighbors call when they witness an individual's risky behavior? A reporting mechanism could supplement CE's assessments and could also begin building the baseline set of indicators needed to establish more effective and automated CE/IT solutions.

- **Finding 7: There are several privacy concerns for CE programs related to sharing personal or privileged individual data.** It might be difficult for key stakeholders to accept a CE security process because there is still no foolproof method of detecting insiders.

- **Recommendation 7: Study standards and establish authorities for access to all relevant nonfederal information that could inform the CE tool, such as local criminal records, mental health information, and significant financial activity.** In addition to the above recommendation, effective CE will also require information connections to nonfederal organizations, which will provide additional access to personally identifiable information (PII).

- **Finding 8: The current investigation and adjudication process is time consuming, creating a large backlog of investigations and periodic reinvestigations.** As of 2018, there were approximately 416,000 unprocessed security clearance investigations and approximately 156,000 unprocessed periodic reinvestigations. Various disturbances have doubled and tripled the time to process each clearance, which contributes to the backlog of incomplete investigations and adjudications.

- **Recommendation 8: Prioritize resources and clearance reviews that present the most urgent investigative and adjudicative issues.** Incorporating a prioritizing mechanism into CE could reduce the inefficiencies of the clearance review process. The backlog of unprocessed periodic reinvestigations could be significantly diminished; the allocation of resources could be more routinely reevaluated and adjusted to accommodate changes in the volume, variety, and scope of investigations.

- **Finding 9a: The organization that has had primary security clearance investigating responsibility has faced resource reductions.** OPM has experienced resource reductions, limiting the office's ability to grow its workforce to address the backlog. OPM estimated the cost of a Tier 3 Secret clearance in 2018 at approximately $430 per person and the cost of a Tier 5 Top Secret clearance at approximately $5,596 per person.

- **Finding 9b: The cost over the long term for CE might be lower than the cost over the same period using current practices.** Current investigations impose rising costs, while CE is estimated to be more cost-efficient in the long term. The greatest costs of the clearance process relate to Top Secret clearances, and this is where the greatest savings occur with CE. Some organizations, such as the State Department, do not even have the data necessary to estimate current costs. While exact costs and savings depend on CE packages selected and population size, estimates revealed that savings might be realized after six years and could be substantial over a longer period.

- **Recommendation 9: Conduct a detailed cost-benefit analysis to determine projected programmatic costs.** Such an analysis should include a detailed comparative breakdown of initial and ongoing costs of the current program and of potential programs that include various aspects of CE. The creation of the National

Background Investigations Bureau by Executive Order 13467 has brought significant improvements to the current security clearance process; however, additional steps could be taken to ensure continued efforts at identifying and reducing costs of the investigative and adjudicative process. An overall assessment of the current security clearance process that looks for areas where CE would accelerate periodic reinvestigations, at no cost to their quality, is necessary. There are likely certain areas, such as aspects of the review process, clearance levels, and types of classified areas, where introducing CE processes would address the most stifling backlogs and costs while ensuring that careful review of critical information remains a central focus of reinvestigations.

- **Finding 10: Despite concerns over personal privacy, CE may be less invasive for the cleared population than current approaches.** The substance of the data CE reviews is not new; only the frequency with which the data are reviewed is. Those individuals receiving greater scrutiny would be limited to those that the CE system identified as having an issue worthy of further investigation, as opposed to all individuals in the entire cleared population.
- **Recommendation 10: Articulate what CE is and is not.** Such a plan should emphasize that while the process of CE is new, the substance is not, and, thus, if executed properly, CE is no more invasive than current processes.

- **Recommendation 11 (overarching): Connect all insider threat information (e.g., security, general counsel, human resources, chief information officer, and other related efforts) to counter insider threats.** Fully implement security clearance reciprocity and suitability/fitness reciprocity among U.S. government departments and agencies and merge the security clearance and suitability/fitness programs and processes to improve coordination and gain maximum vetting value from collected data across programs, departments, and agencies. This would limit the greatest benefit from PII to those involved with CE programs. Those who implement CE programs should have concrete examples of whether additional PII data would bolster insider detection. Available data on previous cases of insider threats should be shared with all those who would benefit from it. Another aspect of this should focus on a better explanation of CE efforts holistically; stakeholders would benefit from a greater understanding that CE intends to remain within the same investigative scope and would only increase the frequency with which individuals are screened. This recommendation, however, represents an ideal for information-sharing to produce more effective CE processes. This study did not consider the broader organizational implications of this recommendation, which would require additional research.

Acknowledgments

The authors would like to thank Sarah Meadows, Christopher Mouton, John Bordeaux, and Stephen Cambone for their very helpful reviews of this report; John Parachini and Rich Girven for providing the opportunity to undertake this exploratory research; and, finally, the government and private-sector subject-matter experts and our RAND colleagues for their time and valuable insights provided during discussions for this study.

Please attribute any errors or omissions solely to the authors.

Abbreviations

ACES	Automated Continuous Evaluation System
ANACI	Access National Agency Check with Inquiries
ARC	Automated Records Checks
CE	continuous evaluation
CERT	Community Emergency Response Team
CM	continuous monitoring
DAS	Data Analytics Supercomputer
DHS	Department of Homeland Security
DITMAC	DoD Insider Threat Management Analysis Center
DoD	U.S. Department of Defense
DOHA	Defense Office of Hearing and Appeals
EAM	Enterprise Audit Management
EO	Executive Order
GAO	Government Accountability Office
IARPA	Intelligence Advanced Research Projects Activity
IC	Intelligence Community
IDES	Intrusion Detection Expert System
IEM	Inference Enterprise Model
INSA	Intelligence and National Security Alliance

IP	intellectual property
IRTPA	Intelligence Reform and Terrorism Prevention Act of 2004
IT	information technology
JRE	Joint Reform Effort
MERIT	Management and Education of the Risk of Insider Threat
NACLC	National Agency Check with Law and Credit
NCSC	National Counterintelligence and Security Center
NISPOM	National Industrial Security Program Operating Manual
NITTF	National Insider Threat Task Force
NSTISSAM	National Security Telecommunications and Information Systems Security Advisory Memorandum
ODNI	Office of the Director of National Intelligence
OIG	Office of Inspector General
OPM	Office of Personnel Management
OUSD(I)	Office of the Under Secretary of Defense for Intelligence
PAC	Performance Accountability Council
PERSEREC	Defense Personnel and Security Research Center
PII	personally identifiable information
SCI	Sensitive Compartmented Information
SCITE	Scientific Advances to Continuous Insider Threat Evaluation
SSBI	single-scope background investigation
TRSS	Thomson Reuters Special Services
UAM	user activity monitoring
UIT	unintentional insider threat
USIS	U.S. Investigations Services

CHAPTER ONE

Introduction

The Traditional Security Clearance Process

At the end of fiscal year 2014, approximately 4.5 million Americans, roughly 1.5 percent of the total population, held a current security clearance in the United States.[1] Specifically, this refers to individuals who have Tier 3 or Tier 5 clearances, according to the Office of Personnel Management's (OPM's) categorization.[2] Each of these individuals underwent some form of background investigation to obtain their clearance. The security clearance process used to grant these clearances has its roots in statutes and executive orders dating back to the Second World War, typically with an eye on perceived levels of loyalty.[3] The process still maintains many of the same structural features, relying heavily on interviews with groups expected to know the candidate well, such as neighbors, friends, and work colleagues. Modern relationships and the periodic reinvestigation process, however, do not always reveal crucial information to a clearance adjudicator.[4] Time, cost, and effectiveness are three critical areas leading the government to consider continuous evaluation (CE) as a more efficient and effective alternative. As will be discussed, definitions of CE vary by industry and organization, but they emphasize the shift from periodic evaluations to a model of continuous monitoring.

---

[1] Office of the Director of National Intelligence (ODNI), *2014 Report on Security Clearance Determinations*, April 2015.

[2] Tier 3 includes individuals with access to noncritical sensitive information at the Confidential and Secret classification levels. Tier 5 designates those with Top Secret and Sensitive Compartmented Information (SCI) clearance levels who also undergo a single-scope background investigation (SSBI). Tiers 1, 2, and 4 are associated with positions without access to classified information that undergo National Agency Check with Inquiries investigations to determine suitability.

[3] William Henderson, "A Brief History of the U.S. Personnel Security Program," ClearanceJobs.com, June 29, 2009.

[4] Scott Stewart, "The Problem with Background Investigations," *Stratfor*, July 4, 2013.

There have been various periods of backlogs in clearance processing;[5] however, the current backlog is particularly large. In 2016, there were approximately 343,557 unprocessed Secret clearance investigations, 72,566 unprocessed Top Secret clearance investigations, and 156,172 unprocessed periodic reinvestigations.[6] Disruptions, such as the 2014 removal of U.S. Investigations Services (USIS), the largest field contractor for OPM; the hack of OPM databases that was revealed in 2015; and numerous other leaks (such as by Chelsea Manning, Edward Snowden, and Reality Winner) contribute to the backlog.[7] These types of disturbances doubled and tripled the time to process each clearance.[8] Additionally, OPM has experienced resource reductions, negatively affecting the office's ability to grow its workforce to address the backlog.[9] In an attempt to address this, the Office of the Undersecretary of Defense for Intelligence (OUSD[I]) signed a memorandum in January 2017 extending the reinvestigation period for individuals holding Top Secret clearances from five years to six.[10]

Cost is another factor to consider. OPM estimated the cost of a Tier 3 Secret clearance in 2018 at approximately $430 per person and the cost of a Tier 5 Top Secret clearance at approximately $5,596 per person.[11] Not all organizations provide estimates for cost and the time it takes to receive a security clearance. For example, the State Department's Office of Inspector General (OIG) published a report in July 2017 noting that a great deal of State's data was incomplete, inconsistent, or inaccurate, leaving the OIG incapable of estimating the time or cost required to process a clearance.[12]

In addition to the time and direct costs required to conduct clearance investigations and adjudications, many question the effectiveness of periodic reinvestigations. A 2014 report conducted after the Navy Yard shooting found that OPM's automated

---

[5]   See comments by David Berteau, president and chief executive officer of the Professional Services Council, the largest trade organization representing government contractors, in Peter Suciu, "What Is the Real Impact of the Security Clearance Backlog?" ClearanceJobs.com, March 27, 2017.

[6]   Data are as of the end of the third quarter in fiscal year 2016 (Charles S. Clark, "Government Warms to Continuous Monitoring of Personnel with Clearances," *Defense One*, July 10, 2017).

[7]   See OPM, "Statement of Kathleen McGettigan, Acting Director, U.S. Office of Personnel Management, Before the Committee on Oversight and Government Reform, United States House of Representatives, on Improving Security and Efficiency at OPM and the National Background Investigations Bureau," February 2, 2017, and Suciu, 2017.

[8]   OPM, *Agency Financial Report: Fiscal Year 2016*, November 2016, p. 12.

[9]   OPM, 2016.

[10]   Office of the Under Secretary of Defense, "Extension of Periodic Reinvestigation Timelines to Address the Background Investigation Backlog," Washington, D.C., January 17, 2017.

[11]   Michelle J. Sutphin, "NISPPAC Security Policy Updates," briefing, National Industrial Security Program Policy Advisory Committee, updated October 9, 2017.

[12]   Office of Inspector General, *Evaluation of the Department of State's Security Clearance Process*, U.S. Department of State, July 2017.

processes, intended to facilitate faster processing of clearances, might have prevented critical investigation information from reaching the adjudicator.[13] The company responsible for the shooter's investigation—USIS—also performed the background investigation on Edward Snowden. The Department of Justice determined in 2014 that USIS "filed at least 665,000 flawed background checks between March 2008 and September 2012, which was about 40 percent of total submissions."[14]

Current processes for investigations are taking longer, are costlier, and might not reveal information that is critical to determine the suitability of an individual for a security clearance, increasing the risk of insider threat (i.e., when an authorized individual uses their access to negatively affect their organization or national security). Conducting these investigations (the frequency of which recently changed to every six or ten years, depending on the clearance level) can contribute to the backlog and, more importantly, could allow future insider threats to develop during the intervening years between investigations. CE could represent a way to address these existing and future issues related to security review process. This study aims to assess CE approaches in hopes of informing leaders in the U.S. Department of Defense (DoD), the U.S. Intelligence Community (IC), and other federal government departments and agencies as they consider insider threats and whether to replace or augment the current security clearance investigation and adjudication process.

Methodology

RAND researchers sought to assess the efficiency and effectiveness of CE through the review of documents and literature on insider threats and CE and interviews with experts from areas involved in ongoing efforts to improve the process. Specifically, the report addresses the following research questions: What capabilities exist to combat insider threat? What aspects of CE are being implemented to address insider threats? What are some costs and benefits of CE? What could be considered in the future? We focused on three sectors: the government, industry, and academia.

We examined documents and peer-reviewed academic journals and conference reports that modeled insider threats, detailed technological and behavioral threat indicators, and outlined physical protection measures mitigating the problem of insider threats. For example, the Carnegie Mellon University Software Engineering Institute's Community Emergency Response Team (CERT) Division presented case studies on insider information technology (IT) sabotage and cybercrimes that provided relevant

---

[13] Darrell Issa, Chairman, Committee on Oversight and Government Reform, "Slipping Through the Cracks: How the D.C. Navy Yard Shooting Exposes Flaws in the Federal Security Clearance Process," Staff Report, Committee on Oversight and Government Reform, U.S. House of Representatives, 113th Congress, February 11, 2014, p. 2.

[14] Sakthi Prasad, "U.S. Brings Fraud Charges Against Firm That Vetted Snowden," Reuters, January 23, 2014.

data to our research. We also surveyed documents, including handouts, general aware-ness pamphlets, and threat checklist brochures distributed by the Federal Bureau of Investigation, the Defense Security Service, and other U.S. government law enforce-ment and security agencies. These documents provided general indicators and precau-tionary steps in identifying insider threats, although they did not offer meaningful substance in addressing our research questions.

We also reviewed the literature on various CE approaches, considered CE cost estimates, examined efficacy and best practices, and assessed some of the practicalities of employing CE.

As a first step, we began with a baseline review of relevant executive orders (EOs), legislative requirements, and policy memorandums outlining access to, reform of, and safeguards for classified information. See Table 1.1 for a list of these documents, along with their date of publication and focus.

The team then surveyed additional insider threat and CE policies and regula-tions issued through open-source DoD guidance, IC guidance, service branch–specific doctrine, and official OPM and Performance Accountability Council (PAC) reports. In addition, we reviewed other documents, including newspapers, magazines, online media, and publicly available comments addressing ongoing efforts of the federal gov-ernment to address insider threat and CE programs.

Finally, we conducted more than a dozen semistructured interviews with subject-matter experts to assist with guiding and scoping our research. We interviewed select U.S. government and private-sector subject-matter experts and RAND experts knowl-

Table 1.1
Primary Documents for Insider Threat and Continuous Evaluation Standards

Base Document	Date	Focus
Public Law 108-458, Intelligence Reform and Terrorism Prevention Act of 2004 (IRTPA), December 17, 2004.	2004	Required annual report of key measurements of the timeliness of the security clearance process
EO 13467, *Reforming Processes Related to Suitability for Government Employment, Fitness for Contractor Employees, and Eligibility for Access to Classified National Security Information*	2008	Reformed suitability standards for government employment processes and eligibility for access to classified national security information, calls for end-to-end automation to the extent practicable, and ensures that relevant information maintained by agencies can be accessed and shared rapidly across the executive branch
EO 13587, *Structural Reforms to Improve the Security of Classified Networks and the Responsible Sharing and Safeguarding of Classified Information*	2011	Outlined reforms to improve the security of classified networks and the responsible sharing and safeguarding of classified information and established the National Insider Threat Task Force (NITTF)
National Insider Threat Policy and Minimum Standards for Executive Branch Insider Threat Programs	2012	Set the standards for executive branch insider threat programs

edgeable in CE and insider threat. We selected outside experts who could provide valuable steering and scoping of the project from the perspective of the federal government.

Based on findings to our research questions (What capabilities exist to combat insider threat? What aspects of CE are being implemented to address insider threats? What are some costs and benefits of CE? What could be considered in the future?), we developed conclusions and recommendations for federal departments and agencies. We have divided this report into six chapters. In this first chapter, we have provided an introduction that briefly discusses the current security process and provides our methodology. Next, in Chapter Two, we expand on the definitions and descriptions of insider threat and CE. In Chapter Three, we provide background and ask three questions about the origins of CE and insider threat, the uniformity of insider threats, and the role that negligence plays regarding insider threats. Chapter Four discusses some capabilities, such as behavioral measures, best practices, and technical measures, that exist to combat insider threats. Chapter Five discusses how CE is being implemented by various sectors and some successes thus far. Finally, in Chapter Six, we provide some concluding comments for consideration.

CHAPTER TWO

Insider Threat and Continuous Evaluation Defined

Our research of CE begins from a definitional perspective. Although the U.S. government has a definition of CE, CE is a relatively new process and, thus, is a new term without a definition in statute.

Insider Threat

There is no commonly shared definition of an insider threat across all three sectors we studied—the government, industry, and academia. The term *insider threat* has taken on different meanings at various times and across different industries. We have categorized these different forms of insider threat for the government into three general types. The first type of threat involves trusted insiders, such as Edward Snowden, Chelsea Manning, and others, who have stolen classified data and released those data for known and unknown reasons.[1] The second type of insider threat comes in the form of espionage against the United States; examples include Aldrich Ames, Robert Hansen, and Ana Montes. This threat to national security through the compromise of classified and other sensitive data belonging to the United States is more insidious because the results are not known unless the perpetrator is caught, and the ramifications of the espionage might never be fully understood. Finally, the third type of insider threat involves the physical violence against individuals. Cleared insiders in agencies across the federal government (such as U.S. Army Major Nidal Hasan, who killed 13 and injured more than 30 at Fort Hood, Texas; U.S. Navy civilian Aaron Alexis, who killed 12 and wounded three at the Washington Navy Yard; and U.S. National Guardsman Esteban Santiago, who killed five in an airport in Fort Lauderdale, Florida) highlight the fact that those in the employ of the United States and who have gone through

---

[1] Mark Berman, "Chelsea Manning on Leaking Information: 'I Have a Responsibility to the Public,'" *Washington Post*, June 9, 2017.

background investigations to serve in positions of trust may still potentially commit heinous acts against their fellow workers.[2]

The White House defines *insider threat* as

> [t]he threat that an insider will use her/his authorized access, wittingly or unwittingly, to do harm to the security of the United States. This threat can include damage to the United States through espionage, terrorism, unauthorized disclosure of national security information, or through the loss or degradation of departmental resources or capabilities.[3]

The definition of *insider threat* by the Department of Justice nearly mirrors this definition.[4]

The ODNI National Counterintelligence and Security Center (NCSC) states:

> An insider threat arises when a person with authorized access to U.S. Government resources, to include personnel, facilities, information, equipment, networks, and systems, uses that access to harm the security of the United States. Malicious insiders can inflict incalculable damage. They enable the enemy to plant boots behind our lines and can compromise our nation's most important endeavors.[5]

The NCSC goes on to say:

> Over the past century, the most damaging U.S. counterintelligence failures were perpetrated by a trusted insider with ulterior motives. In each case, the compromised individual exhibited the identifiable signs of a traitor—but the signs went unreported for years due to the unwillingness or inability of colleagues to accept the possibility of treason.[6]

Finally, the NCSC concludes:

> Insiders convicted of espionage have, on average, been active for a number of years before being caught. Today more information can be carried out the door on removable media in a matter of minutes than the sum total of what was given to our enemies in hard copy throughout U.S. history. Consequently, the damage

---

[2]   Billy Kenber, "Nidal Hasan Sentenced to Death for Fort Hood Shooting Rampage," *Washington Post*, August 28, 2013; and Elise Viebeck and Cleve R. Wootson Jr., "Fort Lauderdale Suspect Claimed Government Was Controlling His Mind Months Before Shooting," *Washington Post*, January 8, 2017.

[3]   Barack Obama, "National Insider Threat Policy and Minimum Standards for Executive Branch Insider Threat Programs," presidential memorandum, Washington, D.C., November 21, 2012.

[4]   U.S. Department of Justice, DOJ Order 0901, "Insider Threat," approved on February 12, 2014.

[5]   NCSC, "Resources: Top Issues: Insider Threat," undated.

[6]   NCSC, undated.

caused by malicious insiders will likely continue to increase unless we have effective insider threat detection programs that can proactively identify and mitigate the threats before they fully mature.[7]

The DoD Defense Security Service defines *insider threat* as

[a]cts of commission or omission by an insider who intentionally or unintentionally compromises or potentially compromises the ability of the DoD to accomplish its mission. These acts include, but are not limited to, espionage, unauthorized disclosure of information, and any other activity resulting in the loss or degradation of departmental resources or capabilities.[8]

Because the definition of *insider* varies in the three sectors we reviewed, any definition of *insider threat* will invariably vary as well. Table 2.1 depicts how these organizational terms differ by sector.

The sample definitions presented here offer three critical insights.

1. The federal government has focused its definition almost entirely on foreign adversaries and counterintelligence.
2. The private-sector IT and cyber definitions focus on theft of intellectual property (IP) and financial assets and harm to organizational systems.
3. Academia expands from the government and private sector to further define and model potential insider threats. These definitions highlight that the actual insider threat may have *already left* the organization.

What is lacking in these definitions, however, is that insider threats include those wishing to cause physical harm to employees and visitors of the workplace. In this report, we adapt an existing definition of *insider threat* put forth by Carnegie Mellon University and incorporate this physical harm element. Our definition of an insider threat is as follows: "the potential for an individual who has or had authorized access to an organization's assets to use their access, either maliciously or unintentionally, to act in a way that could negatively affect the organization or national security."[9]

---

[7]   NCSC, undated.

[8]   Defense Security Service, "Insider Threats," undated-b.

[9]   Modified from a definition seen at Daniel Costa, "CERT Definition of 'Insider Threat'—Updated," *Insider Threat Blog*, Carnegie Mellon University Software Engineering Institute, March 7, 2017.

Table 2.1
Examples of Different Definitions of Insider Threat by Sector

Federal Government[a]	IT/Cyber/Business Industry	Academia
A person who uses their authorized access to DoD facilities, systems, equipment, information, or infrastructure to damage, disrupt operations, compromise DoD information, or commit espionage on behalf of a Foreign Intelligence Entity[b]	Individuals who were, or previously had been, authorized to use the information systems they eventually employed to perpetrate harm[c]	Members of an organization authorized to access its information system, data, or network with a degree of trust by the organization and who accept a commensurate level of scrutiny by the organization to deter possible abuse of these privileges[d]
One or more individuals with the access and/or inside knowledge of a company, organization, or enterprise that would allow them to exploit the vulnerabilities of that entity's security, systems, services, products, or facilities with the intent to cause harm[e]	Anyone in an organization with approved access, privilege or knowledge of information systems, information services, and missions[f]	Any person that has currently or has previously had authorized access[g]
Any efforts within an environment that are being performed in support of an adversary mission or goal[h]	An employee performing malicious behavior—through sabotage, stealing data or physical devices, or purposely leaking confidential information[i]	A result of accidental, careless, or a lack of understanding of the security policies[j]
The threat that an insider will use her/his authorized access, wittingly or unwittingly, to do harm to the security of the United States[k]	An individual and, more broadly, the danger posed by an individual who possesses legitimate access and occupies a position of trust in or with the infrastructure or institution being targeted[l]	Manifested when human behaviors depart from established policies, regardless of whether it results from malice or disregard for security policies[m]
Acts of commission or omission by an insider who intentionally or unintentionally compromises or potentially compromises DoD's ability to accomplish its mission[n]	An employee or a contractor or someone who has authorized access to an organization's systems and networks and uses that access to create harm or damage or something that's inappropriate against organizational policies[o]	Disgruntled employees, who may seek revenge for a perceived injustice, or greedy employees, who may take advantage of organizational information for their own personal gain[p]

[a] The Intelligence Advanced Research Projects Activity (IARPA) Scientific Advances to Continuous Insider Threat Evaluation (SCITE) program states, "Insider threats are individuals with privileged access within an organization who are, or intend to be, engaged in malicious behaviors such as espionage, sabotage or violence" (IARPA, "Scientific Advances to Continuous Insider Threat Evaluation (SCITE)," undated).

[b] DoD Directive 5240.06, "Counterintelligence Awareness and Reporting (CIAR)," May 17, 2011, Incorporating Change 2, July 21, 2017.

[c] Marisa Reddy Randazzo, Michelle Keeney, Eileen Kowalski, Dawn Cappelli, and Andrew Moore, *Insider Threat Study: Illicit Cyber Activity in the Banking and Finance Sector*, Pittsburgh, Pa.: Carnegie Mellon University Software Engineering Institute, CMU/SEI-2004-TR-021, June 2005.

[d] Frank L. Greitzer, Patrick R. Paulson, Lars J. Kangas, Lyndsey R. Franklin, Thomas W. Edgar, and Deborah A. Frincke, *Predictive Modeling for Insider Threat Mitigation*, Richland, Wash.: Pacific Northwest National Laboratory, PNNL-SA-65204, April 2009.

Table 2.1—continued

[e] Thomas Noonan and Edmund Archuleta, *The National Infrastructure Advisory Council's Final Report and Recommendations on the Insider Threat to Critical Infrastructures*, National Infrastructure Advisory Council, April 8, 2008.

[f] Mark Maybury, Penny Chase, Brant Cheikes, Dick Brackney, Sara Matzner, Tom Hetherington, Brad Wood, Conner Sibley, Jack Marin, Tom Longstaff, Lance Spitzner, Jed Haile, John Copeland, and Scott Lewandowski, *Analysis and Detection of Malicious Insiders*, Bedford, Mass.: MITRE Corporation, 2005.

[g] Michael Kirkpatrick, Elisa Bertino, and Frederick Sheldon, "An Architecture for Contextual Insider Threat Detection," white paper, 2009, pp. 1–11.

[h] Defense Advanced Research Projects Agency, "Broad Agency Announcement: Cyber Insider Threat (CINDER) Strategic Technology Office," DARPA-BAA-10-84, August 25, 2010.

[i] Cisco, "Data Leakage Worldwide: The High Cost of Insider Threats," white paper, San Jose, Calif., March 12, 2014.

[j] Todd Fitzgerald, "The Information Security Auditors Have Arrived, Now What?" in Harold F. Tipton and Micki Krause, eds., *Information Security Management Handbook*, New York: Auerbach Publications, 2009.

[k] Obama, 2012.

[l] Nick Catrantzos, *Tackling the Insider Threat*, Alexandria, Va.: ASIS Foundation, CRISP Report, 2010.

[m] Frank L. Greitzer, Christine Noonan, Lars J. Kangas, and Angela Dalton, *Identifying At-Risk Employees: A Behavioral Model for Predicting Potential Insider Threats*, Richland, Wash.: Pacific Northwest National Laboratory, PNNL-19665, September 30, 2010.

[n] Michael Chesbro, *Introduction to Insider Threat: A Summary of Information from Multiple Sources*, Washington, D.C.: U.S. Department of Defense, April 20, 2013.

[o] Booz Allen Hamilton, "The Accidental Insider Threat: Is Your Organization Ready?" panel discussion, September 25, 2012.

[p] Andrew P. Moore, David Mcintire, David Mundie, and David Zubrow, "The Justification of a Pattern for Detecting Intellectual Property Theft by Departing Insiders," *Proceedings of the 19th Conference on Pattern Languages of Programs*, Hillside Group, 2012.

NOTE: There were numerous definitions of *insider threat* throughout the literature. This table offers a sample of those definitions.

Continuous Evaluation

CE has been a U.S. government priority since it was mentioned in EO 13467 in 2008 and is an integral part of current insider threat programs.[10] Work on the Automated Continuous Evaluation System (ACES) progressed over two decades before its implementation in 2007.[11] Definitions for CE in the 2000s centered on the general "collection and analysis of information pertinent to assessing whether a person applying for or holding a security clearance meets the national standards for granting that security

---

[10] Executive Order 13467, "Reforming Processes Related to Suitability for Government Employment, Fitness for Contractor Employees, and Eligibility for Access to Classified National Security Information," *Federal Register*, Vol. 73, No. 128, July 2, 2008, pp. 38103–38108.

[11] DHS, "Privacy Impact Assessment for the Automated Continuous Evaluation System (ACES) Pilot," April 9, 2007.

clearance."[12] EO 13467, issued in 2008 and amended in 2016 and 2017, provided the official U.S. government definition for *CE*, pursuant to Sections 1.3(c) and 1.3(d):

> a vetting process to review the background of an individual who has been deter-mined to be eligible for access to classified information or to hold a sensitive posi-tion at any time during the period of eligibility. CE leverages a set of automated record checks and business rules to assist in the on-going assessment of an indi-vidual's continued eligibility. CE is intended to complement continuous vetting efforts.[13]

This definition highlights that CE is intended to work in conjunction with cur-rent investigation and reinvestigation processes and does not imply a replacement of the current system.

Definitions of CE have not changed substantially despite simultaneous prolifera-tion of technology, such as micro-storage devices, and the advent of social media. Con-fusion between definitions, such as *user activity monitoring* (UAM), *enterprise audit management* (EAM), and *continuous monitoring* (CM), necessitated a Committee on National Security Systems report to clarify the terms.[14] See Table 2.2 for descriptions of these three types of monitoring. The Committee on National Security Systems concluded in 2013 that CE is "the process implemented to maintain a current security status for one or more information systems or the entire suite of information systems on which the operational mission of the enterprise depends."[15]

Much like the case of insider threats, there is no common definition of CE shared between the three sectors we reviewed. Although commonalties exist, attempts to define CE across the defense, intelligence, and private sectors vary. In 2015, the Government Accountability Office (GAO) released a report examining insider threats that contained one section on CE.[16] GAO interviewed six DoD components: three combat support agencies, one military service, one combatant command, and one ser-

---

[12] DHS, 2007.

[13] Executive Order 13764, "Amending the Civil Service Rules, Executive Order 13488, and Executive Order 13467 to Modernize the Executive Branch-Wide Governance Structure and Processes for Security Clearances, Suitability and Fitness for Employment, and Credentialing, and Related Matters," *Federal Register*, Vol. 82, No. 13, January 23, 2017, pp. 8115–8129.

[14] NITTF, *Clarification of Enterprise Audit Management (EAM), User Activity Monitoring (UAM), Continuous Monitoring, and Continuous Evaluation*, NITTF-2014-008, March 2014.

[15] NITTF, 2014.

[16] GAO, *Insider Threats: DoD Should Strengthen Management and Guidance to Protect Classified Information and Systems*, Washington, D.C., GAO-15-544, June 2015.

Table 2.2
National Insider Threat Task Force Categories of Continuous Evaluation

EAM	UAM	CM
Identifying, assessing, deciding on responses to, and reporting on the efficiencies of threats that affect the operational continuance of functionality. Not intended to collect, report, or otherwise act on specific analysis of employee threat behaviors.	Gathering detailed and substantive content about behavioral activity, which may be indicative of an insider threat	Determining whether planned, required, and deployed security controls within information systems or inherited by the system continue to be effective over time, considering the inevitable changes that occur (one of six steps in the Risk Management Framework)

SOURCE: NITTF, *Clarification of Enterprise Audit Management (EAM), User Activity Monitoring (UAM), Continuous Monitoring, and Continuous Evaluation*, NITTF-2014-008, March 2014.

NOTE: The NITTF memorandum states that these core capabilities (EAM, UAM, CM) collectively contribute to overall "system security" and "insider threat detection" programs.

vice subcommand.[17] The report found that the service components needed a "policy that addresses continuous evaluation."[18] Table 2.3 contains GAO findings by entity.

Private industry definitions have been adopted from U.S. government definitions, while the defense and intelligence agencies listed above have working definitions of CE. For example, a series of Intelligence and National Security Alliance (INSA) papers examining insider threats notes that there are two subdivisions of CE. Per Committee on National Security Systems Instruction No. 4009, *continuous monitoring* is defined as "the process implemented to maintain a current security status for one or more information systems or the entire suite of information systems on which the operational mission of the enterprise depends."[19] INSA has opted to combine both variants into a single term—continuous monitoring and evaluation—to emphasize its "belief that workplace Information Technology (IT) use behavior and external personnel data can and should both be defined as inputs to a continuous monitoring process."[20] Other private cybersecurity industry firms have drawn directly from EO 13467 when refining CE methods.[21]

---

[17] GAO selected these six components "based on several factors including their specific roles in supporting DOD networks, prior insider-threat incidents, and reported progress in implementing insider-threat programs" (GAO, 2015).

[18] GAO, 2015.

[19] As cited in INSA, *Leveraging Emerging Technologies in the Security Clearance Process*, March 2014.

[20] INSA, 2014.

[21] See, for example, Cyber Security & Information Systems Information Analysis Center, "Insider Threat Workshop," July 2013, and EY, "Managing Insider Threat: A Holistic Approach to Dealing with Risk from Within," 2016.

Table 2.3
GAO Report Findings by Government Entity

Organization	Findings
DoD	Reviews the background of an individual who has been determined to be eligible for access to classified information (including additional or new checks of commercial databases, government databases, and other information lawfully available to security officials) at any time during the period of eligibility to determine whether that individual continues to meet the requirements for eligibility for access to classified information[a]
Service components	U.S. Army: Involves the uninterrupted assessment of an individual for retention of a security clearance or continuing assignment to sensitive duties; includes reinvestigation at given intervals based on the types of duties performed and level of access to classified information[b]
	U.S. Marine Corps: The reporting of information or behavior that may impact eligibility to hold a clearance, have access to classified information, or the abilities to perform sensitive duties should be included[c]
	U.S. Air Force: Enhancing technical capabilities to monitor and audit user activity on information systems[d]
IC	Include efforts in the security clearance reform process to modernize personnel security processes and increase the timeliness of information reviewed between periodic reinvestigation cycles; supplements and enhances, but does not replace, established personnel security processes by leveraging automated records checks to assist in the ongoing review of an individual's eligibility for access to classified information or to hold a sensitive position[e]

SOURCE: GAO, 2015.

[a] DoD uses the definition set forth in EO 13467 of June 30, 2008. See DoD Instruction 5200.02, "DoD Personnel Security Program (PSP)," March 21, 2014, Incorporating Change 1, Effective September 9, 2014.

[b] Personnel Security, "Continuous Evaluation," undated.

[c] Marine Corps Installations East–Marine Corps Base Camp Lejeune, "What Is Continuous Evaluation?" undated.

[d] Air Force Instruction 16-1402, "Operations Support Insider Threat Program Management," August 5, 2014.

[e] ODNI, "Continuous Evaluation—Overview," undated.

Findings and Recommendations

Finding 1: There is no commonly shared definition of *insider threat* **across the government.** The federal government has focused its definition of insider threat almost entirely on foreign adversaries and counterintelligence. The private sector IT and cyber definitions focus on theft of intellectual property and financial assets and harm to organizational systems. Academia expands from the government and private sector to further define and model potential insider threats. These definitions highlight that the actual insider threat may have *already left* the organization.

Recommendation 1: Establish a common definition of *insider threat* **to facilitate intragovernmental efforts, such as "the potential for an individual who has or had authorized access to an organization's assets to use their access, either**

maliciously or unintentionally, to act in a way that could negatively affect the organization or national security." Because insiders have used their trusted access to the workplace to injure and kill employees and others, the definition should clarify that insider threats include those wishing to cause physical harm to employees and visitors to the workplace. This could include both intent and negligence among the terms that determine an insider's capacity to threaten, injure, kill, or harm employees and to undermine national security interests and infrastructure.

Finding 2: Neither CE nor insider threat has been defined in statute. Although commonalties exist, attempts to define both CE and insider threat across the defense, intelligence, and private sectors vary. A 2015 GAO report found that the service components needed a policy that addresses CE.

Recommendation 2: Establish a common definition of *CE*, such as "a vetting and adjudication process to review on an ongoing basis the background of an individual who has been determined eligible for access to classified information or to hold a sensitive position at any time during the period of eligibility." As with most definitions, it is important that the definition of CE is consistent with its application. There are likely benefits to having a common definition of insider threat and CE programs across the public and private sectors. Any future developments in the definition or application of CE should also extend to both the public and private sectors.

Conclusions

Definitions for insider threat and CE vary among industries and will likely continue to evolve. In this report, we define *insider threat* as "the potential for an individual who has or had authorized access to an organization's assets to use their access, either maliciously or unintentionally, to act in a way that could negatively affect the organization or national security."[22] We define *CE* as "a vetting process to review the background of an individual who has been determined to be eligible for access to classified information or to hold a sensitive position at any time during the period of eligibility."[23]

---

[22] Modified from a definition seen at Costa, 2017, and RAND Corporation, "Security Mandatory Annual Refresher Training (SMART) 2016 Security Training Presentation," undated.

[23] EO 13764, 2017.

CHAPTER THREE

Background: Addressing Insider Threats

In this chapter, we provide readers with background on how the concept of insider threat arose and developed within the U.S. government through an examination of official U.S. legislation, academic journals, and other open-source material. We do this by answering three queries: (1) When did the United States first consider insider threats and CE? (2) Are insider threats uniform across industry? (3) Does the U.S. government consider security negligence a form of insider threat?

When Did the United States First Consider Insider Threats and Continuous Evaluation?

The discussion of CE as related to U.S. national security was evident in the literature we reviewed as early as 1987.[1] DoD Memorandum 5200.2-R noted, "it is not possible at a given point to establish with certainty that any human being will remain trustworthy" with regard to evaluating continued security eligibility.[2] Furthermore, "there is the clear need to assure that, after the personnel security determination is reached, the individual's trustworthiness is a matter of continuing assessment."[3] This DoD document mandated U.S. agencies responsible for the administration of security clearance programs to "establish and maintain a program designed to evaluate [personnel] on a continuing basis."[4] By 1995, EO 12968 expanded the CE concept alerting all clearance holders that "all employees shall be subject to investigation . . . at any time during

---

[1] DoD Memorandum 5200.2-R, "Personnel Security Program," January 1987.

[2] DoD Memorandum 5200.2-R, 1987.

[3] DoD Memorandum 5200.2-R, 1987.

[4] Interestingly, the document also mandated that coworkers also have a duty to report adverse information and clearance holders to supervisors. See DoD Memorandum 5200.2-R, 1987.

the period of access to ascertain whether they continue to meet the requirements for access."[5]

A classification system was developed to explain that the security threat posed by insiders depended on several things, including access to systems, knowledge, security privileges, level of skill, willingness to assume risk, tactics, motivation, and process.[6] Title III of IRTPA required that agencies submit an annual report to Congress of "key measurements as to the timeliness of the security clearance process in February of each year through 2011."[7] IRTPA also called for the use of a consolidated database bolstered by emerging technology to expedite investigations, verify ongoing suitability, and augment periodic reinvestigations.[8]

The U.S. government understood that it quickly needed a way to track progress toward meeting security clearance goals outlined in IRTPA—especially as supporting technologies generated increasing amounts of data. EO 13467 established the PAC in 2008. The PAC was to drive "implementation of the reform effort, ensuring accountability by agencies," and ensure that the "Suitability Executive Agent and the Security Executive Agent align their respective processes" to sustain "reform momentum."[9] Regarding suitability, fitness, and eligibility to access classified information, EO 13467 also called for the creation of an aligned system to

> employ updated and consistent standards and methods, enable innovations with enterprise information technology capabilities and end-to-end automation to the extent practicable, and ensure that protecting privacy-related information, ensuring resulting decisions are in the national interest, and providing the Federal Government with an effective workforce.[10]

EO 13587 formally established the NITTF in 2011 in response to the leak of classified information to WikiLeaks by Manning.[11] The NITTF was charged with

---

5   Executive Order 12968, "Access to Classified Information," *Federal Register*, Vol. 60, No. 151, August 7, 1995, pp. 40245–40254.

6   B. Wood, "An Insider Threat Model for Adversary Simulation," in *Proceedings of the Research on Mitigating the Insider Threat on Information Systems, August 30–September 1*, No. 2, Arlington, Va., 2000.

7   ODNI, "IRTPA Title III Annual Report for 2010," February 15, 2011.

8   Public Law 108-458, 2004.

9   EO 13467, 2008.

10   "End-to-end automation" means an executive branch–wide federated system that uses automation to manage and monitor cases and maintain relevant documentation of the application (but not an employment application), investigation, adjudication, and continuous evaluation processes." See EO 13467, 2008.

11   Executive Order 13587, "Structural Reforms to Improve the Security of Classified Networks and the Responsible Sharing and Safeguarding of Classified Information," October 7, 2011. See also Kyle Ebersole, "Continuous Evaluation: Welcoming Government Employees to the World of Mass Surveillance," *George Mason Law Review*, Vol. 23, No. 2, 2016, pp. 445–477.

developing a program to deter, detect, and mitigate insider threats and safeguard classified information from "exploitation, compromise, or other unauthorized disclosure, taking into account risk levels, as well as the distinct needs, missions, and systems of individual agencies."[12] In 2012, the White House released the *National Insider Threat Policy and Minimum Standards for Executive Branch Insider Threat Programs*, which provided individual agencies the

> elements necessary to establish effective insider threat programs. These elements include the capability to gather, integrate, and centrally analyze and respond to key threat-related information; monitor employee use of classified networks; provide the workforce with insider threat awareness training; and protect the civil liberties and privacy of all personnel.[13]

The *Suitability and Security Processes Review Report to the President* in 2014 attempted to operationalize CE by providing the PAC authority to administer "real-time access to authoritative enterprise data on the conduct of investigations and the adjudicative decisions from across the government."[14] To accomplish this task, the PAC drew on best practices from ongoing CE efforts of ODNI, DoD, and OPM.

Following EO 13587 and the *National Insider Threat Policy and Minimum Standards for Executive Branch Insider Threat Programs*, DoD released the *National Industrial Security Program Operating Manual (NISPOM) Change 2*, a 2016 revision to the previous 2006 document. The policy pertains specifically to contractors, outlining requirements to "establish and maintain an insider threat program that will gather, integrate, and report relevant and available information indicative of a potential or actual insider threat."[15]

Are Insider Threats Uniform Across Industry?

The literature on insider threats has evolved from describing threats in black-and-white terms—either a threat or not—to identifying threats across a spectrum. Rather than "binary" distinctions of whether someone is or might be an insider threat, there are

---

[12] This program included the development of "policies, objectives, and priorities for establishing and integrating security, counterintelligence, user audits and monitoring, and other safeguarding capabilities and practices within agencies."

[13] Obama, 2012.

[14] Performance Accountability Council, *Suitability and Security Processes Review: Report to the President*, February 2014.

[15] U.S. Department of Defense, *National Industrial Security Program Operating Manual*, DoD 5220.22-M, February 2006, Incorporating Change 2, May 18, 2016, p. 1-2-1.

instead "attackers with varying degrees and types of access."[16] Access can be defined as the "ability to perform actions allowed by one policy level but disallowed at a higher policy level, or vice versa," leading to the various degrees of "insiderness."[17]

Organizations have offered an array of definitions when attempting to define the insider threat problem, and so the term *insider* has taken a variety of forms. Incidents over the past decade (e.g., Manning, Snowden, Hasan) allowed the security industry to sort insiders by intent. For example, *malicious insiders* are "trusted insiders that intentionally steal data for their own purpose," *careless and negligent insiders* are "people within or directly associated with the organization that do not have malicious intent," and *compromised insiders* "allow external threats to act with the same level of freedom as the trusted insider itself."[18] The latter two categories highlight two instances of insiders not normally associated with insider acts; rather than committing intentional, malicious acts, these insiders are forcibly coerced by an external actor—or simply do not adhere to security protocols.

Additionally, the National Security Telecommunications and Information Systems Security Advisory Memorandum (NSTISSAM) of 1999 offered four "insider categories" for consideration: (1) A *traitor* is a person who has a malevolent intent to damage, destroy, or sell out their organization; (2) a *zealot* is an insider who believes strongly in the correctness of one position or feels that the organization is not on the right side of a certain issue; (3) a *browser* is overly curious in nature and may violate the need-to-know principle; and (4) a *well-intentioned* insider commits violations through ignorance.[19] We think it prudent to add a fifth category, the *violent insider*, to account for violence in the workplace. While there are many different versions of these four categories within the literature, the NSTISSAM provided the basis for refined categorizations to the present. See Figure 3.1 for the five types of insiders.

Does the U.S. Government Consider Security Negligence a Form of Insider Threat?

Across the government, agencies acknowledge that accidents and negligence can pose an insider threat. The 2009 Information Security Management Handbook found that "the insider threat because of accidental, careless, or a lack of understanding of the

---

[16]   Matt Bishop, Sophie Engle, Deborah A. Frincke, Carrie Gates, Frank L. Greitzer, Sean Peisert, and Sean Whalen, "A Risk Management Approach to the 'Insider Threat,'" in Christian W. Probst, Jeffrey Hunker, Dieter Gollmann, and Matt Bishop, eds., *Insider Threats in Cyber Security*, Boston, Mass.: Springer, 2010, pp. 115–137.

[17]   Bishop et al., 2010.

[18]   Imperva, *Insiders: The Threat Is Already Within*, Hacker Intelligence Initiative Report, Redwood Shores, Calif., 2016.

[19]   National Security Telecommunications and Information Systems Security Advisory Memorandum, "The Insider Threat to U.S. Government Information Systems," INFOSEC/1-99, July 1999.

Figure 3.1
Five Types of Insiders

The Traitor	The Zealot	The Browser	The Well-Intentioned	The Violent Insider
"malicious insider" (Maybury et al., 2005) *"disgruntled insider"* (Cisco, 2014) *"active insider"* (IAEA, 2008) *"malicious user"* (Caputo and Stephens, 2009) *"trusted insider"* (Shaw, Fischer, and Rose, 2009) *"infiltrator"* (Catrantzos, 2010)	*"hacktivist"* (Ludlow, 2010) *"idealist"* (Cyber Security & Information Systems Information Analysis Center, 2013)	*"passive insider"* (IAEA, 2008)	*"unintentional insider"* (CERT Insider Threat Team, 2013) *"non-malicious insiders"* (Cyber Security & Information Systems Information Analysis Center, 2013) *"careless and negligent insiders"* (Imperva, 2016)	*"the active shooter"* *"the lunatic"* *"the deranged"* (RAND Corporation, 2016)

"There is no single profile that fits all cases."
(Buford, 2008)
"No single threat assessment technique gives a complete picture of the insider threat problem."
(Greitzer et al., 2009)

SOURCES: Data from NSTISSAM, 1999, and RAND analysis.

security policies should also be regarded as the insider threat."[20] The Department of Homeland Security (DHS) Science and Technology Directorate Cyber Security Division states that an insider threat "can be defined as the potential violation of system security policy by an authorized user."[21] The CERT Insider Threat Team further studied whether unintentional insider threats (UITs) posed an actual threat.[22] Research by CERT revealed that "more than 40% of computer and organizational security professionals report that their greatest security concern is employees accidentally jeopardizing security through data leaks or similar errors."[23]

---

[20] Fitzgerald, 2009.

[21] DHS Science and Technology Directorate Cyber Security Division, "Insider Threat," March 3, 2016.

[22] CERT Insider Threat Team, "Unintentional Insider Threats: A Foundational Study," Pittsburgh, Pa.: Carnegie Mellon University Software Engineering Institute, technical report, 2013.

[23] UIT should be entirely preventable, given strict classified information safeguards in place, but it still frequently occurs as individuals within an organization look to cut corners or actively disregard security policies (CERT Insider Threat Team, 2013).

Findings and Recommendations

Finding 3: While the U.S. government has thought about insider threats for many years, threats over the past decade, such as Manning, Snowden, and Hasan, have provided momentum in attempts at resolving those threats. These cases and others led to categorizing insider threats by intent as opposed to considering them exclusively on a binary scale as threats or not threats.

Recommendation 3: Given that insider threats exist across a broad spectrum, it would be useful to categorize insider threats in attempting to reduce and mitigate them. Intent is often an explicit threat indicator among insider categories; by contrast, negligence is not. While negligence does not necessarily imply intent, negligence, as committed by insiders who fall under the *well-intentioned* category, for example, should also be considered a threat because it introduces serious liability and consequences.

Conclusions

While the U.S. government has thought about insider threats for decades, recent threats (e.g., Manning, Snowden, Hasan) have spurred new momentum. These types of cases have changed the method for categorizing insider threats from a binary distinction to a more flexible and comprehensive method that categorizes by intent, which accounts for variation in the degree and type of access an insider holds, as well as the scope and nature of physical, fiscal, and informational harm that a threat can pose.

CHAPTER FOUR

What Capabilities Exist to Combat Insider Threats?

In this chapter, we review the current technological, behavioral, and physical mechanisms meant to deter and detect would-be insider threats. We answer three questions: (1) What are some best practices to combat insider threats? (2) Could behavioral measures be used to combat insider threats? (3) How are technical measures used to combat insider threats?

What Are Some Best Practices to Combat Insider Threats?

The methods employed by the industries we examined are best administered through a wide range of organizational functions. The existing literature suggests that, despite differences between the various industries (i.e., government, commercial, and academic), many best practices for the CE of insider threats are common across industry. The RAND team has considered four categories of best practices based on commonality.

- First, we identify the role of risk assessment, which helps organizations think about what is worth protecting and the characteristics of compromising behaviors and actions of potential threats.
- Next, we discuss the role of organizational culture as a safeguard against insider threats. Periodic education can be deployed to foster and enhance this culture. We will discuss how commitment of executives and functional leaders can improve this culture and, thus, the monitoring and evaluation process.
- Third, we examine threat monitoring best practices.
- Finally, this section explores some of the robust security policies enacted across industry that are used to control behaviors and actions of insiders to reduce vulnerabilities. This is accomplished through a review of the key elements of a security infrastructure that organizations can use to combat internal and external threats.

Risk Assessment

Organizations must first identify and classify assets that are worth protecting to help focus the scope of an insider threat program.[1] This will determine the degree of risk and the types of threat incidents that are likely to be associated with each asset.[2] Continually updating this list will help define and redistribute resources as needed.[3] Certain assets, such as intellectual property, are inherently more at risk than others. Next, organizations must survey and understand the threat landscape. The National Security Institute found that over 70 percent of network espionage cases occur from the inside.[4] This suggests that organizations should dedicate significant resources to determine who has access to valued information, what devices and systems are used to process this information, and what types of behaviors and characteristics are associated with threats to these assets.[5] A risk assessment should also establish a baseline of normal activity for each position, making it easier to catch anomalies and thereby triggering an investigation.[6] Assigning risk levels to every position within the organization can help assess the degree of vetting necessary for each new candidate and the degree of continuous monitoring once they are deemed trustworthy.[7]

Research indicates that many insider threat issues arise from disgruntled employees.[8] A report on insider risk highlights the importance of profiling employees and keeping data on "predispositions," and "behaviors of concern."[9] These behaviors can be social behaviors, such as employee-to-employee discussions regarding the damage one can inflict on an organization's IT systems, or technical actions, such as accessing files or information that are outside the purview of one's role. Organizations should consider factors that shape employee behavior and make them vulnerable to attack. For example, an employee can become disgruntled because of a lack of opportuni-

---

[1]   Raytheon, "Best Practices for Mitigating and Investigating Insider Threats," 2009.

[2]   Raytheon, 2009.

[3]   CERT Insider Threat Center, *Common Sense Guide to Mitigating Insider Threats, Fifth Edition*, Pittsburgh, Pa.: Carnegie Mellon University Software Engineering Institute, CMU/SEI-2015-TR-010, December 2016.

[4]   National Security Institute, *Improving Security from the Inside Out: A Business Case for Corporate Security Awareness*, Medway, Mass., 2004.

[5]   CERT Insider Threat Center, 2016.

[6]   DHS, "National Cybersecurity and Communications Integration Center, Combating the Insider Threat," May 2, 2014; Stephen R. Band, Dawn M. Cappelli, Lynn F. Fischer, Andrew P. Moore, Eric D. Shaw, and Randall F. Trzeciak, *Comparing Insider IT Sabotage and Espionage: A Model-Based Analysis*, Pittsburgh, Pa.: Software Engineering Institute, Carnegie Mellon University, CMU/SEI-2006-TR-026, December 2006.

[7]   CERT Insider Threat Center, 2016.

[8]   Deanna D. Caputo and Gregory D. Stephens, "Detecting Insider Theft of Trade Secrets," Bedford, Mass.: MITRE Corporation, November/December 2009.

[9]   Eric D. Shaw, Lynn F. Fischer, and Andrée E. Rose, *Insider Risk Evaluation and Audit*, Monterey, Calif.: Defense Personnel Security Research Center, Technical Report 09-02, August 2009.

ties for raises and promotions, thus affecting the threat landscape.[10] The CERT team recommends developing a "risk-indicator instrument for the assessment of behaviors and technical actions related to potential risk" of insider threats.[11] CERT recommendations also explain the need for "improved data on the relative distribution, interrelationships, and weight with respect to attack risk of concerning behaviors, stressful events, and personal predispositions."[12] Gathering data on employee predisposition, however, may cause friction with privacy laws and other organizational norms in place to keep records confidential. Any system that gathered this type of information would have to ensure the integrity and security of the data so that it could not be used for purposes other than CE adjudication.

Culture and Education

Safety and security are not the responsibilities of any one department or functional team in an organization; instead, they should be internalized by each member of an organization.[13] This can be difficult because employee beliefs may not necessarily align with organizational values and, as such, may not prioritize protecting information.[14] Periodic education can help foster this security consciousness. Management can communicate the significance of and reasons for security policy through education and training courses. One Cisco report found that "43 percent of IT professionals said they are not educating employees well enough."[15] Training should be continuous, beginning with new hires, and should continue to reinforce concepts and to maintain working knowledge of the threat environment.[16] Prominent insider threat examples, such as the case of Reality Winner, can narrow perception and awareness of the varying archetypes of the insider threat. Awareness training should encompass these archetypes along with the range of behaviors and skill sets of known insider threats, including UITs.[17] Employees should learn "to recognize phishing and other social media threat vectors" that prey on their trust and technical ignorance.[18] This heightened awareness must be coupled with a mechanism that allows employees to report suspicious or compromis-

---

[10] George Silowash, Dawn Cappelli, Andrew Moore, Randall Trzeciak, Timothy J. Shimeall, and Lori Flynn, *Common Sense Guide to Mitigating Insider Threats, Fourth Edition*, Pittsburgh, Pa.: Carnegie Mellon University Software Engineering Institute, 2012.

[11] Band et al., 2006.

[12] Band et al., 2006.

[13] Cisco, 2014.

[14] "Five Habits of Companies That Catch Insiders," Dark Reading, October 22, 2012.

[15] Cisco, 2014.

[16] Cisco, 2014, and CERT Insider Threat Team, 2013.

[17] CERT Insider Threat Center, 2016.

[18] CERT Insider Threat Team, 2013.

ing activity anonymously.[19] Organizations should implement a training program for all levels of employees, including executives and senior management, to underscore the significance of security training.

An effective security culture means complete participation from the top down to the least-trusted insider. Senior management could set the tone for the organization and should be active in communicating security policy to the rest of the workforce.[20]

Threat Monitoring

Organizations can use data from risk assessments to build an insider threat monitoring system. An effective threat monitoring system uses the knowledge of possible threat incidents to determine how they might trigger investigative policies. Raytheon has identified typical triggers for investigations in the areas of data loss, theft, leaks of intellectual property, fraud, abuse by privileged users, and policy compliance.[21] Employees who have been fired or asked to resign or who have voluntarily resigned should be closely monitored during the following month to ensure that they do not exploit existing credentials to access sensitive material. CERT describes numerous cases in which departing employees have sought access and stolen information for personal gain or have brought former company secrets to their next job. Termination of access and associated credentials, such as passwords and identification badges, at the point of separation is crucial in protecting the organization.[22] Network user activity logs also provide data to mine and analyze when a trigger is set.[23] Having a complete set of data points will give greater insight into actions leading up to a trigger and reduces the risk of chasing false positives and accidental behaviors.[24] Organizations should also log all incidents, regardless of impact, to build more effective databases for analysts that can be used to learn, refine, and develop new indicators and trigger points.[25]

---

[19]   CERT Insider Threat Center, 2016.

[20]   Fitzgerald, 2009.

[21]   Raytheon, 2009.

[22]   Michael Hanley and Joji Montelibano, *Insider Threat Control: Using Centralized Logging to Detect Data Exfiltration Near Insider Termination*, Pittsburgh, Pa.: Carnegie Mellon University Software Engineering Institute, CMU/SEI-2011-TN-024, October 2011; Band et al., 2006.

[23]   Raytheon, 2009; Fitzgerald, 2009; CERT Insider Threat Center, *Common Sense Guide to Mitigating Insider Threats, Fifth Edition*, Pittsburgh, Pa.: Carnegie Mellon University Software Engineering Institute, CMU/SEI-2015-TR-010, December 2016.

[24]   Raytheon, 2009.

[25]   Raytheon, 2009; Fahmida Y. Rashid, "Learn from Past Incidents," *eWeek*, March 5, 2012; George Silowash, "Building an Insider Threat Program: Five Important Categories of Tools (Part 1 of 2)," *Insider Threat Blog*, Carnegie Mellon University Software Engineering Institute, July 26, 2016.

Security Policy and Infrastructure

A robust security policy is necessary for any organization looking to safeguard its physical space and information systems. Effective security policies should be enforced during hiring and termination processes.[26] Preemployment screening will help determine the integrity and trustworthiness of any candidate seeking to become an insider.[27] The employee termination process should include the shutdown of accounts, as well as access to the physical space and information systems, to "reduce the risk of damage from former employees."[28] This further highlights the importance of the risk assessment phase, which determines the physical hardware and system accesses granted to each position, leading to a quick termination of accesses by system administrators. In addition, this type of assessment helps in the implementation of the least privilege rule, which grants access to information or facilities only to those who need it to perform their work function, thereby limiting the amount of damage any one insider can inflict.[29]

Organizations should implement strong password protections on user accounts to bolster the effectiveness of the least privilege rule.[30] Managers should instruct users not to write down or share their passwords with others. This is not just a matter of protecting the organization but also self-preservation. One can envision a scenario in which an insider uses a colleague's credentials and triggers an investigation that is attributed to the unwitting victim. Organizations should communicate these policies to their members continually to reinforce ideas, concepts, and rationale while providing updates. Communicating the policies effectively means striking a balance between robustness and simplicity.[31]

Another safeguard against internal and external threats is the implementation of system change controls. These controls are designed to protect the integrity of information and restrict access to information by an individual user.[32] If an insider does successfully compromise an information system by changing settings or removing data, a mature security infrastructure should be able to restore the system settings and data using backup files and controls.[33] There will always be system administrators who need

---

[26] Fitzgerald, 2009.

[27] International Atomic Energy Agency, *Preventive and Protective Measures Against Insider Threats Implementing Guide*, Vienna, IAEA Nuclear Security Series No. 8, 2008.

[28] CERT Insider Threat Center, 2016; Fitzgerald, 2009.

[29] Fitzgerald, 2009; CERT Insider Threat Center, 2016.

[30] For information on strong passwords, see Cybersecurity and Infrastructure Security Agency, "Security Tip (ST04-002): Choosing and Protecting Passwords," last revised November 21, 2018. Also see Fitzgerald, 2009; and CERT Insider Threat Center, 2016.

[31] Cisco, 2014.

[32] CERT Insider Threat Center, 2016.

[33] Fitzgerald, 2009; CERT Insider Threat Center, 2016.

permissions to manipulate a significant portion of the system, despite attempts to limit and compartmentalize access to information throughout the overall workforce. System administrators and other technical experts account for many insider threat cases.[34] Although it is difficult to guard against these types of users, organizations can create processes that require two users to make critical modifications to the system or data. The system administrator position is based on an elevated level of trust, and organizations need to remain vigilant against threats from this position.

Could Behavioral Measures Be Used to Combat Insider Threats?

Insider threats are people—not machines. Current research on the topic of CE emphasizes the implementation of behavioral data in conjunction with traditional cybersecurity to shift from threat detection to threat prediction.[35] One recent INSA report explained that, because the insider threat develops within individuals, "organizations must identify psychosocial events—anomalous, suspicious, or concerning nontechnical behaviors."[36] According to a 2012 article, "a survey of 40 companies that have successfully dealt with insider threats shows that the solution is less technology and more psychology."[37] Furthermore, organizations that build "close relationships" with their employees have had "greater success at protecting their businesses' valuable data."[38] While there are no foolproof behavioral indicators, our research results derived from the literature suggest some best practices for consideration when adopting behavioral traits into a CE program.

Current research on CE emphasizes implementation of behavioral data in conjunction with traditional cybersecurity to shift away from threat detection toward threat prediction.[39] Several qualitative and quantitative behavioral models were adopted over the past decade to address precursor insider threat traits. A summary of these models is presented in Table 4.1.

The various behavioral approaches adopted share one major challenge: There are limited data available to test the reliability of such studies. This has created the need to adopt alternative sociobehavioral theories. Insider threats are especially difficult

---

[34]   CERT Insider Threat Center, 2016.

[35]   Frank L. Greitzer and Deborah A. Frincke, "Combining Traditional Cyber Security Audit Data with Psychosocial Data: Towards Predictive Modeling for Insider Threat Mitigation," in Christian W. Probst, Jeffrey Hunker, Dieter Gollmann, and Matt Bishop, eds., *Insider Threats in Cyber Security*, Boston, Mass.: Springer, 2010, pp. 85–113.

[36]   Intelligence and National Security Alliance Cyber Council, "Insider Threat Task Force," September 2013.

[37]   "Five Habits of Companies That Catch Insiders," 2012.

[38]   "Five Habits of Companies That Catch Insiders," 2012.

[39]   Greitzer and Frincke, 2010.

Table 4.1
Summary of Key Behavioral Models Adapted to Combat Insider Threats

Example Behavioral Models Adopted to Combat Insider Threat Problem	Sources
Counterproductive Workplace Behavior	INSA, *Assessing the Mind of the Malicious Insider: Using a Behavioral Model and Data Analytics to Improve Continuous Evaluation*, April 2017
Five-Factor Model	Goldberg, 1993
Psychological Contract Breach	Ambrose et al., 2002; Folger and Skarlicki, 2005; Pearson and Andersson, 2005; Rosen et al., 2009; Tripp and Bies, 2009; Phelps et al., 2007 (cited in Greitzer et al., 2010)
Social Judgment Theory	Brunswik, 1943; Hammond, 1996; Hammond and Stewart, 2001 (cited in Ignacio J. Martinez-Moyano, Eliot H. Rich, Stephen H. Conrad, and David F. Andersen, "Modeling the Emergence of Insider Threat Vulnerabilities," *Proceedings of the 2006 Winter Simulation Conference*, IEEE, 2006, pp. 562–568)
Signal Detection Theory	Green and Swets, 1966; Swets, 1973 (cited in Martinez-Moyano et al., 2006)
Learning Theory	Erev, 1998; Klayman, 1984 (cited in Martinez-Moyano et al., 2006)
System Dynamics Theory	Forrester, 1961; Richardson and Pugh, 1989; Sterman, 2000 (cited in Martinez-Moyano et al., 2006)
Agent-Based Modeling Theory	Buford, 2008
Sentiment Analysis/Advanced Psycholinguistics	INSA, 2017; Samantha Ehlinger, "Finding Feelings: Intelligence Agency Lines Up New Tool for Rooting Out Insider Threats," FedScoop, February 6, 2017

NOTE: This information in this table was compiled from the RAND team's literature search.

to detect not only because of unique "behavioral and cognitive traits of individuals involved in the process" but also associated "high levels of uncertainty, incomplete and imperfect information, incomplete and delayed feedback, and low base rates."[40]

Behavioral problems and detection are frustrated by myriad factors:

- Actors may already have legitimate access and, as such, do not need to engage in illegal behavior to exfiltrate sensitive information.[41]

---

[40] Ignacio J. Martinez-Moyano, Eliot H. Rich, Stephen H. Conrad, and David F. Andersen, "Modeling the Emergence of Insider Threat Vulnerabilities," *Proceedings of the 2006 Winter Simulation Conference*, IEEE, 2006, p. 563. Martinez-Moyano expanded on factors related to learning behavior in 2008; see Ignacio J. Martinez-Moyano, Eliot Rich, Stephen Conrad, David F. Andersen, and Thomas R. Stewart, "A Behavioral Theory of Insider-Threat Risks: A System Dynamics Approach," *ACM Transactions on Modeling and Computer Simulation*, Vol. 18, No. 2, Article 7, April 2008.

[41] Deanna D. Caputo, Greg Stephens, Brad Stephenson, and Minna Kim, "Human Behavior, Insider Threat, and Awareness: An Empirical Study of Insider Threat Behavior," Bedford, Mass.: MITRE Corporation, technical

- Machine-generated events must be filtered manually before user behavior can be analyzed.[42]
- Limited access to offenders has inhibited ongoing research efforts; behavioral analysts have not been able to gain any thorough understanding of the psychology of an insider.[43]

Greitzer's work on the predictive behaviors of insider threats offers three points of consideration for understanding future insider threat barriers, given the access limitations that researchers have faced in understanding the problem.[44]

- First, proactive insider threat approaches must identify a full range of precursor behaviors or characteristics that insider threats may exhibit, such as personal stressors and work disgruntlement.[45] This information will provide managers avenues through which to address personal employee grievances to divert malicious behavior. Because behavioral indicators may erroneously imply the likelihood of an attack, it is important to retain this human element in any automated behavior program. Table 4.1 displays some examples of the types of precursors that may be indicative of a growing insider threat.
- Second, there are ethical and privacy considerations to consider when instituting behavioral programs. Combining cybersecurity data with unique PII data may infringe on civil liberty and privacy protections. Organizations implementing CE/IT programs will need to weigh any proactive measure, such as continuous monitoring, that might further contribute toward individual satisfaction with the working environment.[46]
- Third, legacy CE and insider threat anomaly detection systems have failed to detect insiders because automated parameters set by organizations may be scoped too rigidly and because, over time, such systems may begin to treat repeated anomalies as a normal baseline. This will require organizations that institute CE

---

paper, February 2010.

[42] Caputo et al., 2010. Also see Caputo and Stephens, 2009.

[43] For example, Charney writes that insiders that are imprisoned are "out of reach to researchers, except for those who work within the intelligence community or for those who work for private companies that have been cleared for such studies." See D. L. Charney, "True Psychology of the Insider Spy," *Intelligencer: Journal of the U.S. Intelligence Studies*, Vol. 18, No. 1, 2010, pp. 47–54.

[44] Greitzer et al., 2009; Frank L. Greitzer, Deborah A. Frincke, and Mariah Zabriskie, "Social/Ethical Issues in Predictive Insider Threat Monitoring," in Melissa Jane Dark, ed., *Information Assurance and Security Ethics in Complex Systems: Interdisciplinary Perspectives*, Hershey, Pa.: IGI Global, 2010, pp. 132–161; Greitzer and Frincke, 2010; and Greitzer et al., 2010.

[45] Greitzer et al., 2009.

[46] Greitzer, Frincke, and Zabriskie, 2011.

policies to draw from a wider range of precursor psychological and motivational factors.[47]

INSA has also examined a number of behavioral models in its continuing efforts to improve CE.[48] INSA found that "certain personality traits may predispose an employee to acts of espionage, theft, violence, or destruction."[49] INSA issued a report in April 2017 that examined how such traits could be monitored through personality mapping—e.g., psycholinguistic tools, life event detection (such as data-mining social media networks), and emotion detection (i.e., sentiment analysis).[50] Experts suggest that insiders are not formed "overnight,"[51] which confirms Greitzer's point that a broad spectrum of behavioral analytics could help highlight derogatory personal information not normally contained within the current security clearance and suitability process.[52]

How Are Technical Measures Used to Combat Insider Threats?

Technological developments play a large role in efforts to mitigate insider threats. Such techniques rely on one or more of four traditional intrusion detection systems: threshold, anomaly, rule based, and model based.[53] These systems are similar because they provide large-scale, automated checks based on patterns of activity and audit user records to monitor potential threats. Unlike other aspects of CE that monitor individual behavior to make assessments about the reliability or suitability of the individual, these technical measures inform the CE review process while at the same time protecting systems and information through real-time detection of malicious or unusual behavior. Threshold detection and anomaly detection are early detection techniques and are a form of summary statistics. For example, an "alarm goes off because someone enters the wrong password ten times in a row."[54] This is the most basic of the four methods. It sets a reasonable baseline of activity and monitors user deviations. The other three methods rely on more-advanced algorithms to detect potential malicious activity. Anomaly detection is generally broken down into two types: profile based and

---

[47] Frank L. Greitzer and Ryan E. Hohimer, "Modeling Human Behavior to Anticipate Insider Attacks," *Journal of Strategic Security*, Vol. 4, No. 2, June 2011, p. 25.

[48] INSA, 2017.

[49] INSA, 2017.

[50] INSA, 2017.

[51] INSA, 2017.

[52] Greitzer and Hohimer, 2011.

[53] Chet Langin and Shahram Rahimi, "Soft Computing in Intrusion Detection: The State of the Art," *Journal of Ambient Intelligence and Humanized Computing*, Vol. 1, No. 2, 2010, pp. 133–145.

[54] Langin and Rahimi, 2010, p. 135.

rule based. An *anomaly intrusion* is defined as "being based on anomalous behavior.[55] The Intrusion Detection Expert System (IDES) is generally considered the standard for statistical profile-based anomaly detection.[56] IDES uses a profile-based component that compares actual behavior to expected behavior based on user, group, remote host, and target system criteria.[57] Rule- and signature-based methods also exist, but these "are limited to work within the bounds of the defined signature database."[58] Additionally, with these methods, "variations of known signatures are easily created to thwart such misuse-detectors, and completely novel attacks will nearly always be missed."[59] There is also a model-based detection technique: "Model-based methods seek to recognize attack scenarios at a higher level of abstraction than the other approaches, which largely focus on audit records exclusively as data sources."[60] This is the most advanced technique because it allows users to generate and model potential intrusions to fit the needs of internal networks.[61]

Technological defenses employed in the CE context range from basic use of IT access controls and software to more-nuanced methods and models that allow for dynamic and preemptive approaches. A fundamental approach of preventing inappropriate data exfiltration is the use of tools that centrally log and monitor web-based services in near-real time to protect sensitive information. For example, firewall log entries are used to identify network problems and detect malware that could be used to exfiltrate system information.

Government entities have drawn from preexisting techniques in other sectors and have tailored these approaches to combat insiders. For example, the Defense Advanced Research Projects Agency Cyber Insider Threat program uses CE techniques borrowed from the private sector and has since increased the "accuracy, rate and speed with which insider threats are detected and impede the ability of adversaries to operate unde-

---

[55] Langin and Rahimi, 2010, p. 135.

[56] Koral Ilgun, Richard A. Kemmerer, and Phillip A. Porras, "State Transition Analysis: A Rule-Based Intrusion Detection Approach," *IEEE Transactions on Software Engineering*, Vol. 21, No. 3, 1995, pp. 182–183; E. D. Shaw and L. F. Fischer, "Ten Tales of Betrayal: The Threat to Corporate Infrastructures by Information Technology Insiders Analysis and Observations," Monterey, Calif.: Defense Personnel Security Research Center, 2005; Greitzer, Frincke, and Zabriskie, 2011; and P. Lenca, P. Meyer, B. Vaillant, and S. Lallich, "On Selecting Interestingness Measures for Association Rules: User Oriented Description and Multiple Criteria Decision Aid," *European Journal of Operational Research*, Vol. 184, No. 2, 2008, pp. 610–626.

[57] Ilgun, Kemmerer, and Porras, 1995, p. 183; and H. S. Javitz and A. Valdes, "The SRI IDES Statistical Anomaly Detector," in *Proceedings of the IEEE Symposium on Research in Security and Privacy*, May 1991, pp. 316–376.

[58] Frank L. Greitzer and Thomas A. Ferryman, "Methods and Metrics for Evaluating Analytic Insider Threat Tools," *Proceedings of the 2013 IEEE Security and Privacy Workshops*, 2013, p. 90; Ilgun, Kemmerer, and Porras, 1995.

[59] Greitzer and Ferryman, 2013, p. 90; Ilgun, Kemmerer, and Porras, 1995.

[60] Greitzer and Ferryman, 2013, p. 90.

[61] Ilgun, Kemmerer, and Porras, 1995.

tected within government and military interest networks."[62] The DoD Insider Threat Management Analysis Center (DITMAC) was created in response to the Washington Navy Yard shooting of 2013. DITMAC now "provides a centralized capability that can quickly analyze the results of automated records checks and reports of behavior of concern and recommend action as appropriate."[63]

Organizations must tailor their use of technical methods to fit their needs while providing protection from the variety of threats that could arise. In one recent example, CERT found that an individual is most likely to steal intellectual property within 30 days of termination.[64] CERT outlined a pattern that organizations should follow within that 30-day window before termination to appropriately monitor departing employees, based on this information. Result of the study led to two separate models to increase the monitoring of departing employees.[65]

Findings and Recommendations

Finding 4: There are limited behavioral or technical data available to develop and deploy an effective and predictive CE monitoring tool. Scholars and practitioners of CE have been forced to develop technical solutions based on generalized behavioral indicators because access to actual insider threats and their associated data streams is not available. Without ground-truth data on past incidents and behaviors, effective anomaly detection can only be modeled. There have been some attempts to marry behavioral and technological CE efforts within the U.S. IC, but limitations, such as receiving too many false alarms, coupled with a lack of risk indicators to feed IT detections systems provide little value in mitigating actual threats.

Recommendation 4: Conduct a thorough academic and scientific review of behavioral approaches that predict insider threat behavior before it occurs. The federal government, private sector, and academic community should work together to develop an effective way to share the unique data and behavioral traits gained from actual insider cases. In cases in which access is limited about the actual insiders, inves-

---

[62] Defense Advanced Research Projects Agency, 2010.

[63] Defense Security Service, "DoD Insider Threat Management and Analysis Center," undated-a.

[64] Michael Hanley, Tyler Dean, Will Schroeder, Matt Houy, Randall F. Trzeciak, and Joji Montelibano, *An Analysis of Technical Observations in Insider Theft of Intellectual Property Cases*, Pittsburgh, Pa.: Carnegie Mellon University Software Engineering Institute, CMU/SEI-2011-TN-006, February 2011.

[65] The two models were the Entitled Independent Model and the Ambitious Leader Model. The key to knowing which model to use was considering behavioral aspects of the employee in conjunction with the implementation of increased monitoring. See Andrew P. Moore, Michael Hanley, and David Mundie, *A Pattern for Increased Monitoring for Intellectual Property Theft by Departing Insiders*, Pittsburgh, Pa.: Carnegie Mellon University Software Engineering Institute, CMU/SEI-2012-TR-008, April 2012.

tigative field notes and interrogation reports may provide the descriptors necessary to build a more effective program.

Finding 5: Public- and private-sector organizations have experienced an increase in the number of insider threat incidents in the period surrounding an employee's termination. The 30-day period both before and after an employee has left an organization is critical and requires increased focus for CE programs. There are notable instances of insiders looking to cause damage in the event of nonvoluntary separation and other instances in which employees have taken organizational intellectual property to bring to their next job.

Recommendation 5: Increase the frequency of continuous monitoring efforts surrounding the period of an employee's termination in both public- and private-sector CE programs. Continuous monitoring programs, by their nature, will occur more frequently than currently established OPM and other agency security clearance readjudication processes. However, future CE implementation should ensure that this frequency is increased in termination situations. In addition, there may be other similar instances (e.g., notable life changes, negative coworker reports or evaluations) in which the frequency of CE must be increased.

Finding 6: There is no centralized or authorized facility to receive anonymous reporting streams for individuals in either cleared or uncleared populations. We noted the lack of a formalized reporting mechanism that could be used to supplement CE processes. For example, family members, coworkers, or neighbors might be aware of or witness individual events that many times go unreported during the standard security, suitability, and fitness processes.

Recommendation 6: Create a real-time reporting mechanism to supplement any future security clearance approach, including one involving CE. This might assist in preventing the next Fort Hood shooting, WikiLeaks upload, or insider-espionage ring. Who should close family members or neighbors call when they witness an individual's risky behavior? A reporting mechanism could supplement CE's assessments and could also begin building the baseline set of indicators needed to establish more effective and automated CE/IT solutions.

Finding 7: There are several privacy concerns for CE programs related to sharing personal or privileged individual data. It might be difficult for key stakeholders to accept a CE security process because there is still no foolproof method of detecting insiders.

Recommendation 7: Study standards and establish authorities for access to all relevant nonfederal information that could inform the CE tool, such as local criminal records, mental health information, and significant financial activity. In addition to the above recommendation, effective CE will also require information connections to nonfederal organizations, which will provide additional access to PII.

Conclusions

The existing literature suggests that, despite differences between the various industries, the best practices for the CE of insider threats are common across industries. These include conducting risk assessments, fostering a work culture of security awareness, building a threat monitoring system based on conducted risk assessments, and building robust security policies and infrastructure. In areas where current practices need improvement, the challenges to enhancing CE are also common across industries. While behavioral components of an insider threat program can strengthen monitoring, most behavioral approaches suffer from the same challenge of limited or no baseline data. Technological approaches already play a large role in efforts to mitigate insider threats, but they cannot prevent, detect, or weaken insider threats alone.

CHAPTER FIVE

How Is Continuous Evaluation Implemented Today?

In this chapter, we examine CE as addressed today and how current efforts might inform the future. We address the following five questions:

1. How do different sectors address insider threat and CE issues?
2. How successful has CE been so far?
3. What are some costs and benefits of CE?
4. What is not CE?
5. What are some challenges to implementing CE?

How Do Different Sectors Address Insider Threats and Continuous Evaluation Issues?

The RAND team performed research and conducted interviews with personnel from DoD, the IC, and the private sector to understand some of the challenges they face and the trends of some of their CE and insider threat programs. The findings list below is not exhaustive but instead serves as a sample of various programs and efforts underway.

U.S. Government Programs
Intelligence Advanced Research Projects Activity
IARPA's SCITE program seeks to "develop and test methods to detect insider threats through two separate research thrusts."[1] The first line of program research has focused on insider threat indicators, while the second line of efforts is developing *inference enterprise models* (IEMs) to "forecast the accuracy of existing and proposed systems for detecting insider threats."[2] Unlike other ongoing pilots, the SCITE program is focused on combining insider threat indicators with a CE tool. Chief information officers are focused on the internal side (IT and networks) of insider threats, while the CE team is

---

[1] In 2017, the SCITE program was one year into a three-year program (IARPA, undated; interview with IARPA program managers, April 2017).

[2] IARPA, undated.

focused on external factors.[3] IARPA program managers have partnered with academia and private industry to develop a list of risk factors and indicators—while separately using three other groups to provide ground-truth data for testing. One major finding from the ongoing SCITE program is that the current systems have been overwhelmed with false alarms.[4] Another limitation is that current technological detectors are not closely associated with risk indicators and have provided "little value" so far, per interviewees.[5] Because SCITE is still in its first year of operation, there have not yet been any qualitative evaluations of the objective indicators that would eventually be needed to quantify current data.

Office of the Under Secretary of Defense for Intelligence

Interviews with intelligence and security staff at DoD revealed that insider threat policies are still reactionary and are not yet aligned with the emerging threat environment.[6] Attempts to bridge insider threat programs with CE components are frustrated by an absence of common working definitions, an outdated framework, and a lack of preemptive technological measures. As of May 2017, DoD had issued two System of Records Notices, one related to the insider threat and the other for CE.[7] The lack of a consistent framework in this area has necessitated two separate legal reviews within DoD. DoD continuously looks to relevant literature for guidance in performing internal cost-benefit and risk analysis of such programs but has been stymied by few applicable case studies. This is an area that would benefit from additional research.

DoD Insider Threat Management and Analysis Center

Interviews with DITMAC personnel confirm that CE and insider threat programs are not as effectively integrated as they could be.[8] DITMAC has had difficulty in conveying the merit of protection versus privacy consideration to its stakeholders. A good CE program will protect employee information and data; however, convincing stakeholders of the utility in voluntarily providing such information has been difficult because there is no current foolproof method of detection. Another potential issue for DITMAC is conveying the value of CE/IT monitoring because there are no variables with which to experiment. The development of metrics for insider threat programs have proven

---

[3]   Interview with IARPA program managers, April 2017.

[4]   Interview with IARPA program managers, April 2017.

[5]   Interview with IARPA program managers, April 2017.

[6]   Interview with OUSD(I) personnel, May 9, 2017.

[7]   "A system of records is a group of any records under the control of any agency from which information is retrieved by the name of the individual or by some identifying number, symbol, or other identifier assigned to the individual. The Privacy Act requires each agency to publish notice of its systems of records in the Federal Register. This notice is generally referred to as a System of Records Notice or SORN" (DHS, "System of Record Notices," undated).

[8]   Interview with DITMAC and OUSD(I) personnel, April 13, 2017.

especially difficult because pilot projects have addressed perceived threats rather than actual ones. DITMAC has assessed the relationship between CE and insider threat programs as one of connecting user activity monitoring and CE. DITMAC is in the testing phase of two primary risk models focused on pre- and post-incident risks. The CE pre-incident risk model uses Bayesian and Haystax modeling to create a daily risk report for top-level managers. This model is in the second phase of pilot testing, with a reported detection accuracy rate of 95 percent. The insider threat pilot, now in its third year of testing, is serving as a risk-triage function to shape mitigation strategies, though this could take another year before intended effects can be implemented.

Private-Sector Efforts
Thomson Reuters Special Services
Thomson Reuters Special Services (TRSS), a company offering services in insider threat and global risk insight, seeks to mitigate insider threats by analyzing "external risk indicators found in public records and open source data to help detect, prevent, and respond to insider incidents."[9] TRSS personnel collect publicly available information and cross-check it through other internal data sources.[10] TRSS personnel explained that the main obstacles in aligning CE and insider threat programs lay in prioritizing department and agency assets, differing protection authorities, quality of information-sharing between agencies, and funding.[11]

TransUnion
TransUnion leverages publicly available and credit bureau data with predictive analysis, analyzing "changes in behavior as leading indicators of threats."[12] Like TRSS, TransUnion cross-checks its financial data with other information, understanding that not all triggers are indicative of an insider threat. For example, someone who suddenly started spending more money might have recently received an inheritance or money from a trust fund.[13] TransUnion personnel suggest that while publicly available information does not include internal data (e.g., human resources data), research has shown the critical role that financial information plays in insider threat mitigation and granting clearances to those who need them.[14]

---

[9]   See TRSS, "Insider Threat," undated.

[10]   Interview with TRSS personnel, June 19, 2017.

[11]   Interview with TRSS personnel, June 19, 2017.

[12]   TransUnion, "Threat Monitoring Solutions: Using Changes in Behavior as Leading Indicators of Threats," 2016.

[13]   RAND interview with TransUnion personnel, June 23, 2017.

[14]   In particular, TransUnion personnel pointed to two different pieces of research. The first is a 2008 study led by Eileen Kowalski. The study found that "financial gain was both the motive for, and objective of, most insiders' illicit cyber activities" (Eileen Kowalski, Tara Conway, Susan Keverline, Megan Williams, Dawn Cappelli, Brad-

LexisNexis

LexisNexis focuses on risk from insiders by leveraging "data about people, businesses, and assets to assess risk and opportunity associated with industry-specific problems."[15] In 2004, LexisNexis offered the services of its Data Analytics Supercomputer (DAS) to government clients to manage, search, and analyze their large volumes of data.[16] The DAS allows LexisNexis to pull different types of structured and unstructured data from multiple sources and refine the data's quality down to the most relevant information for analytics.

How Successful Has Continuous Evaluation Been So Far?

Several CE pilot projects have tested automated system accuracy to supplement periodic reinvestigations for U.S. security clearance holders; however, most reports that could provide an understanding of whether such pilots have added value or the specific direction the pilot projects are taking have not been publicly released. This section surveys pilot programs mentioned in the open press. The RAND team has limited access to ongoing pilot program results; therefore, it is difficult to comment on actual measures, metrics, and findings in practice throughout these DoD and IC pilot programs. As such, this section also provides, where available, pilot project outcome information to aid future CE planning efforts.

Automated Continuous Evaluation System

ACES, developed in 2007 by DoD's Defense Personnel and Security Research Center (PERSEREC), was the first CE pilot program, and it was administered to approximately 20,000 personnel located at DoD headquarters.[17] ACES, developed over a 20-year period,[18] automates the "collection and analysis of information pertinent

---

ford Willke, and Andrew Moore, *Insider Threat Study: Illicit Cyber Activity in the Government Sector*, Pittsburgh, Pa.: Carnegie Mellon University Software Engineering Institute, January 2008, p. 16). The second is from the Defense Office of Hearing and Appeals (DOHA), which "provides hearings and issues decisions in personnel security clearance cases for contractor personnel doing classified work" (DOHA, homepage, 2019). TransUnion analyzed each of the 2016 cases brought before DOHA and found that financial considerations were by the far the most common reason for DOHA denying a security clearance.

[15]   LexisNexis, "Using Identity Management and Predictive Analytics to Prevent Fraud and Improve Provider and Member Management?" February 6, 2013.

[16]   LexisNexis, "Making Sense of Data: The LexisNexis Data Analytics Supercomputer (DAS) Delivers Results," white paper, undated.

[17]   DHS, 2007.

[18]   Katherine L. Herbig, Ray A. Zimmerman, and Callie J. Chandler, *The Evolution of the Automated Continuous Evaluation System (ACES) for Personnel Security*, Seaside, Calif.: Defense Personnel and Security Research Center, Technical Report 13-06, November 2013.

to assessing whether a person applying for or holding a security clearance meets the national standards for granting that security clearance."[19] DoD notes that ACES is not intended to "replace the existing reviews by Office of Security personnel" but instead was developed to supplement existing processes.[20]

There have been two versions of ACES; the first version, rolled out between 2004 and 2009, allowed "computer-to-computer and fully automated" interactions, while other interactions were indirect, in that "a request for data would be sent to data providers who ran the check themselves and sent the resulting data back to an ACES operator."[21] The U.S. government's Joint Reform Effort (JRE) released a report in 2008 recommending that any effective CE program should also focus on collecting and validating "more information about a security clearance applicant early in the process through an expanded electronic application and Automated Records Checks (ARC)."[22] The release of that report changed the course of ACES implementation—shifting to implement the goals laid out by the JRE.[23] ACES would no longer focus solely on CE, but instead ACES outputs would now be integrated into "initial background investigation, and it would reach beyond DoD personnel and contractors to a wider population including other departments of the federal government."[24] Table 5.1 summarizes ACES pilot projects.

Because the outcomes of these various CE pilot programs have not been released to the public, it is difficult to assess the overall impact of the types of efficiencies CE offers in the context of the ACES program and other DoD and IC CE programs. However, the unclassified results (per the final column in Table 5.1) suggest that CE is exhibiting signs of utility in (1) reporting previously unknown information about clearance holders, (2) identifying additional areas of concern for program managers to be monitored, (3) providing data in a timely fashion, and (4) overall cost savings.

---

[19] DHS, 2007.

[20] DHS, 2007.

[21] Herbig, Zimmerman, and Chandler, 2013.

[22] Herbig, Zimmerman, and Chandler, 2013.

[23] Herbig, Zimmerman, and Chandler, 2013.

[24] Herbig, Zimmerman, and Chandler, 2013, also noted,

> Changes in organizational context within DoD were a second important influence shaping ACES. Since DoD had supported and sponsored ACES from its inception, organizational changes in DoD affected ACES' development. Two changes in DoD especially influenced ACES: 1) the transfer of DoD's background investigations to the Office of Personnel Management (OPM) in 2005, and 2) the creation of the Defense Information System for Security (DISS) in 2009. Both of these brought additional players and competing agency interests into ACES development.

Table 5.1
Descriptions and Results of ACES Pilot Projects

Name	Date Range	Participants	ACES Goals	Results
Database Matching Pilot Study	1998–2000	DoD Defense Security Service	This study assessed the feasibility and value of acquiring computerized data from 15 different government and private vendor databases not routinely checked during federal personnel security investigations	The databases evaluated provided information that at least some of the special agents reported was valuable in certain cases; the study helped to identify the rates of issue detection from various data sources being evaluated
Initial Air Force Pilot Study	2002–2003	DoD: Air Force and Defense Intelligence Agency	PERSEREC conducted ACES checks on 14,120 individuals with Air Force Top Secret or SCI access; this was the first pilot study to use "live" data	The study demonstrated that ACES could identify numerous issues of security concern that would be of interest to adjudicators
ACES Beta Test	2004–2005	DoD	ACES was tested by adjudicators at seven DoD Consolidated Adjudications Facilities to evaluate the utility of its reports	Adjudicators reported finding new information or issues of interest in 80.6% of the issue cases detected by ACES and said that they would like to receive similar cases in the future in 84.5% of the cases
DHS Pilot Study	2007–2008	DHS	In this first non-DoD pilot evaluation of ACES, checks were conducted on 12,802 cases provided by the eight DHS components	The study identified issues of concern in 10.7% of the 6,407 initial and periodic reinvestigations and in 4.3% of the 6,395 CE cases; it also identified 27 cases with one or more issues that had been missed in previous investigations
ACES Pilot Study for DHS comparing three ARC strategies for SSBIs with traditional SSBIs	2008	Army SSBIs	This second evaluation of ACES for DHS evaluated the added contribution of commercial electronic data providers to the ACES-based ARC strategy framed in April 2008 by the JRE	The study demonstrated that the incorporation of ACES-based ARC strategies provided cost savings over the traditional SSBI investigations
OPM/ACES Pilot, Phase 1 and Phase 2	2010–2011	Navy National Agency Checks with Law and Credit (NACLCs) and Access National Agency Checks with Inquiries (ANACIs)	Phase 1 was an analysis of a small convenience sample of 400 Army NACLC and ANACI investigations; results from analyzing this sample informed the second phase. Phase 2 focused on investigations and adjudications done on active-duty, civilian, and contract Navy personnel undergoing either an NACLC or an ANACI.	ACES checks proved more timely and less costly for similar issue identification rates in many instances, while OPM traditional checks (which are not directly comparable to ACES checks) identified more issues in other instances

Table 5.1—Continued

Name	Date Range	Participants	ACES Goals	Results
DoD/ODNI ACES Pilot Study DoD/ODNI ACES Pilot Study	2011–2012	Army NACLCs	This study focused on investigations and adjudications of 1,478 Army recruits intended to demonstrate key JRE reform concepts, including the following goals: (1) Demonstrate an end-to-end electronic process from initiation of a personnel security or suitability investigation to adjudication, using existing systems; (2) utilize the eAPP, the U.S. Army Recruiting Command's version of the e-QIP, to complete the SF-86; (3) collect and transmit fingerprints electronically; and (4) evaluate the effectiveness of using ACES in the ARC-based investigation and flagging approach	The overall end-to-end process using existing capabilities was successful, and timeliness goals were achieved; ACES and the SF-86 were the two most productive sources of issue cases
DoD CE Pilot Study	2012	DoD contractor personnel	PERSEREC conducted this study for the JRE to examine ACES in terms of CE as envisioned in the September 2011 Draft Federal Investigative Standards	The traditional SSBI missed 35 cases detected by the ACES-based ARC option, while the ACES-based option missed 23 cases detected by the SSBI
Army CE Pilot Study	2012	Army	The project randomly selected a sample of 4,000 cleared Army personnel and then used PII to conduct checks using ACES, social media queries, and a commercial data provider of public records (bankruptcies, liens, judgments, or jail bookings)	There were 35 revocations and 18 individuals given conditional access; ACES identified significant issues of concern that had not been reported, including 24 individuals with more than $25,000 in unpaid debt; in 13% of issue cases, ACES identified issues in two or more adjudicative categories
DoD Small Army CE Pilot Study	2012	Army	This study determined the utility of ACES checks in the conduct of internal investigations	The Army reported that the results were "useful"

Table 5.1—Continued

Name	Date Range	Participants	ACES Goals	Results
State Department (State) Pilot Study	2013– in progress	State	This study assessed the value of individual ACES records checks as an enhancement to the State investigation or to replace some of the current State investigative leads	No further information
Army Accessions Pilot Study	2013	U.S. Military Entrance Processing Command and U.S. Army Recruiting Command	This study's goal was to provide earlier detection of disqualifying factors, to demonstrate that earlier detection resulted in reduced program and training costs, and to address medical pre-screening conducted by the Military Services through evaluation of electronic health records' existence, accessibility, and automated capability	No further information

NOTES: While the titles of these reports are unclassified, the reports themselves are not generally available to the public. We have omitted report names here, but they can be found in Appendix A of Herbig, Zimmerman, and Chandler, 2013.

Community Emergency Response Team

The CERT Division of Carnegie Mellon's Software Engineering Institute provides additional data points that have affected ongoing insider threat and CE efforts. Although the following CERT publications are not pilot studies themselves, they do offer value to current and future CE pilot project efforts.

CERT's current database offers information related to more than "1,000 insider threat cases" that help CERT to "identify motivations and warning signs."[25] While not exclusively focused on background checks or periodic reinvestigations, CERT works with DHS to set goals in such areas as data collection, trend analysis, and insider threat management.[26] CERT developed a living database in 2006 that is continuously updated with insider threat reporting from the government and the private sector. CERT researchers have explored a variety of topics related to sabotage, espionage, and theft of intellectual property.[27]

One CERT report focused on comparisons between insider IT sabotage and insider espionage cases to assess "whether a single analytical framework based on system

[25] CERT, "About Us," undated.

[26] CERT, undated.

[27] Carnegie Mellon University Software Engineering Institute, "Insider Threat," 2017.

dynamics modeling could be developed to isolate the major factors or conditions leading to both categories of trust betrayal."[28] To draw comparisons, CERT conducted modeling of both domains, finding that, because the insider threat shares "many contributing and facilitating system dynamics features," insider threats "might be detected and deterred by the same or similar administrative and technical safeguards."[29]

Other efforts focused on refining insider threat motivations,[30] identifying common patterns among insider incidents through system dynamics modeling,[31] and identifying indicators for future research.[32] CERT conducted Management and Education of the Risk of Insider Threat (MERIT) modeling using systems dynamics and case study analysis in 2008 of 30 insider IT sabotage incidents to identify "common patterns in the evolution of the cases over time."[33] The case studies and subsequent modeling revealed several observations suggesting that most insiders had personal predispositions that contributed to their risk of committing IT sabotage; most insiders who committed sabotage were disgruntled because of unmet expectations; behavioral precursors were often observable in insider IT sabotage cases but were ignored by the organization; organizations had failed to detect technical precursors; and the majority of insiders attacked after termination.[34]

Other CERT work addressed how insider threats remove IP from the workplace. These studies built on previous work to reduce the risk of IP theft by departing insiders.[35] Such considerations included increased monitoring of employees in the final month before termination, immediately revoking access upon receiving letters of resignation, and reducing "problematic organizational behavior in which excessive trust of insiders can lead to insufficient monitoring, a lack of detection of concerning activities, and even greater trust in potentially misbehaving insiders."[36] A series of three reports analyzed trends of how insiders exfiltrate intellectual property.[37] The top

---

[28] Band et al., 2006.

[29] Band et al., 2006.

[30] Andrew P. Moore, Dawn M. Cappelli, Thomas C. Caron, Eric Shaw, Derrick Spooner, and Randall F. Trzeciak, *A Preliminary Model of Insider Theft of Intellectual Property*, Pittsburgh, Pa.: Carnegie Mellon University Software Engineering Institute, CMU/SEI-2011-TN-013, June 2011.

[31] Andrew P. Moore, Dawn M. Cappelli, and Randall F. Trzeciak, "The 'Big Picture' of Insider IT Sabotage Across U.S. Critical Infrastructures," in Salvatore J. Stolfo, Steven M. Bellovin, Angelos D. Keromytis, Shlomo Hershkop, Sean W. Smith, and Sara Sinclair, *Insider Attack and Cyber Security: Beyond the Hacker*, Boston, Mass.: Springer, 2008, pp. 17–52.

[32] Moore, Hanley, and Mundie, 2012.

[33] Moore, Cappelli, and Trzeciak, 2008.

[34] Moore, Cappelli, and Trzeciak, 2008.

[35] Moore, Hanley, and Mundie, 2012.

[36] Moore, Hanley, and Mundie, 2012.

[37] Hanley et al., 2011.

three methods were by email from the workplace (30 percent), by removable media (30 percent), and by remote network access (28 percent).[38] Half of the cases examined occurred during normal business hours, while 20 percent of insiders attacked outside of normal business hours.[39] Lastly, 62 percent of the incidents occurred on site, whereas 22 percent occurred through remote access.[40] Separate research found that, in many instances, insiders have "stolen information within the 30 days prior to departure."[41]

Another CERT report studied how insiders have increasingly turned to high-tech methods, such as the cloud, for data exfiltration and data manipulation within organizations.[42] This presents in two ways—the insider who "exploits a cloud-related vulnerability to steal information from a cloud system" and the insider who uses cloud systems to carry out an attack on an employer's local resources.[43] These methods can present as an inside "rogue administrator" who steals "sensitive information, resulting in loss of data confidentiality and/or integrity"; an insider who "exploits vulnerabilities exposed by the use of cloud services to gain unauthorized access to organization systems and/or data"; or an insider who uses "cloud services to carry out an attack on his own employer."[44] In contrast, another CERT report, focused on criminal activity within the banking and financial sector, determined that the means employed by the insider were typically not technically sophisticated and that most incidents were detected through an audit, customer complaint, or coworker suspicion.[45]

Finally, Claycomb et al. analyzed 15 insider threat cases of IT sabotage and found that (1) "most saboteurs and spies had common personal predispositions that contributed to their risk of committing malicious acts"; (2) "concerning behaviors were often observable before and during insider IT sabotage and espionage"; (3) "technical actions by many insiders could have alerted the organization to planned or ongoing malicious acts"; and (4) a "lack of physical and electronic access controls facilitated both IT sabotage and espionage."[46]

---

[38]   Hanley et al., 2011.

[39]   Hanley et al., 2011.

[40]   Hanley et al., 2011.

[41]   Hanley and Montelibano, 2011.

[42]   William R. Claycomb and Alex Nicoll, "Insider Threats to Cloud Computing: Directions for New Research Challenges," *2012 IEEE 36th Annual Computer Software and Applications Conference*, IEEE, July 2012.

[43]   Claycomb and Nicoll, 2012.

[44]   Claycomb and Nicoll, 2012.

[45]   Adam Cummings, Todd Lewellen, David McIntire, Andrew P. Moore, and Randall F. Trzeciak, *Insider Threat Study: Illicit Cyber Activity Involving Fraud in the U.S. Financial Services Sector*, Pittsburgh, Pa.: Carnegie Mellon University Software Engineering Institute, CMU/SEI-2012-SR-004, July 2012.

[46]   William R. Claycomb, Carly L. Huth, Lori Flynn, David M. McIntire, and Todd B. Lewellen, "Chronological Examination of Insider Threat Sabotage: Preliminary Observations," *Journal of Wireless Mobile Networks, Ubiquitous Computing, and Dependable Applications*, Vol. 3, No. 4, December 2012, pp. 4–20.

What Are Some Costs and Benefits of Continuous Evaluation?

Private companies, such as those discussed above, currently offer CE alternatives for customers. These packages appear to be customizable, including options for the types of records or data evaluated, types and weights of triggers for the data, use of their analysts to monitor the system, and the frequency and depth of reports conducted.[47] Options exist at different price points, and including larger populations would result in economies of scale, with lower costs per employee. Current estimates, depending on the package selected and population size, can range from $0.20 to $5 per employee per month.[48] Initial costs of setup for the CE system appear to be minimal, particularly if organizations leverage initial background investigations as baselines on current employees.

When we used these estimates, we found that CE could become more cost-effective if use of CE either delayed or reduced the number of periodic reinvestigations required. As discussed previously in this report, the estimated cost of a Tier 3 Secret clearance in 2018 was approximately $433 per person, and the cost for a Tier 5 Top Secret clearance was approximately $5,596 per person.[49] Employees with a Secret clearance must undergo reinvestigation every ten years, and those with a Top Secret clearance now require reinvestigation every six years.[50] This means that the cost of clearance investigations is significant for the initial investigation and then again during these periodic reinvestigations. In contrast, if an employee undergoes an initial background investigation and then is monitored through CE, there would be an initial investigation cost followed by an ongoing CE cost for the organization at a much lower rate. Figure 5.1 shows the costs of a single individual at the liberal estimate of $5 per month for that individual after five years (i.e., before a Top Secret reinvestigation would be required), after six years (i.e., after the Top Secret reinvestigation), after nine years (i.e., before a Secret reinvestigation), after ten years (i.e., after the Secret reinvestigation), after 12 years (i.e., after a second Top Secret reinvestigation), and after a 25-year career.

With approximately 5.1 million clearance holders, of whom approximately 3.6 million hold a Secret clearance and approximately 1.5 million have a Top Secret

---

[47] Discussions with private-sector companies.

[48] This estimate does not include additional costs of in-depth reports on individuals in the case of an employee setting off a trigger. These kinds of reports were estimated at roughly $15–$30 each, per discussions with private-sector companies.

[49] Data on the cost of security clearance process per individual are sporadic. Subsequent briefings from the National Industrial Security Program Policy Advisory Committee from May 2018 and August 2018 did not associate updated costs with SSC processes. These data also do not clarify whether this cost estimate includes man-hours outside of the formal OPM investigation process (Sutphin, 2017).

[50] Requirements for reinvestigations were required by EO 12968, signed August 4, 1995, to be determined by the Security Policy Board. Periodic reinvestigations for Top Secret clearance holders were updated in Office of the Under Secretary of Defense, 2017.

Figure 5.1
Estimated Costs of Continuous Evaluation Versus the Current Review System over Time for One Employee

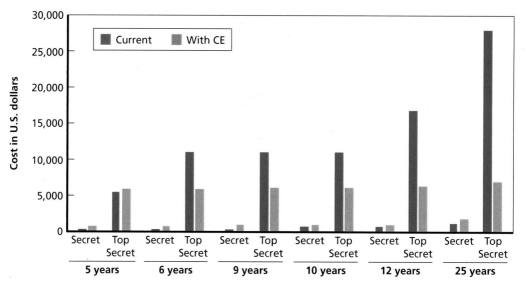

SOURCES: RAND analysis based on data from discussions with private-sector subject-matter experts; Sutphin, 2017.

clearance, the additional cost over 25 years for CE for Secret clearance holders would be approximately $2.16 billion, and the savings would be approximately $30 billion. This equals an estimated savings of $27.84 billion using CE in the security clearance process over a hypothetical 25-year period. The comparative cost for CE is significantly lower for those with a Top Secret clearance because of the added complexity and cost of a Top Secret clearance investigation and adjudication. CE is more expensive for a Secret clearance holder because these employees undergo fewer reinvestigations, but each reinvestigation costs considerably less than a Top Secret clearance. At current estimates, the cost per employee per month would need to be closer to $3.60 to match the cost of the current process for those holding a Secret clearance. This might be possible, depending on the continuous monitoring services provided and the size of the population. We considered a sample of 1 million individuals—the current number in the DoD pilot.[51] Figure 5.1 shows that, with each iteration of reinvestigations, the savings associated with CE grow.

---

[51] As of 2013, there were reportedly 5.1 million Americans holding clearances, with approximately 3.6 million of those being Secret clearances (Brian Fung, "5.1 Million Americans Have Security Clearances. That's More Than the Entire Population of Norway," *Washington Post*, March 24, 2014). We used these numbers instead of the 2014 figure of 4.5 million because they had a better estimation of the ratio of clearance holders.

Most of cost of the clearance process is in Top Secret clearances, and this is where the greatest potential savings with CE exist.

The actual population of roughly 4.5 million cleared Americans is more complex in nature than is presented here. For example, these estimations assume some constants, such as reinvestigation costs, employees remaining at the same level of clearance, and time between each reinvestigation.[52] We used the liberal estimate of $5 per employee per month as a buffer for additional costs potentially incurred, but we did not account in our estimates for in-depth reviews of individuals who are identified by CE as needing additional attention. While these examples do not provide a true number of potential savings in leveraging CE as opposed to reinvestigations, they do suggest that the savings could be substantial.

What Is Not Continuous Evaluation?

This research explored what CE is and how such an approach can be leveraged for evaluating the cleared population. There are important caveats, however, when it comes to what CE is and what it is not. In CE, the *process* is new, but the *substance* is not new. This type of monitoring evaluates a subset of data that is already reviewed for clearance holders, which is primarily publicly available information. Instead, the change is in how often this information is reviewed. Under the current process of reinvestigation, six or ten years can pass without an employee's criminal and financial contacts being reviewed. Instead, CE turns backward-looking investigations into a current, constant review, creating opportunities for organizations to find potential threats sooner.

This foundation of CE's nature leads to two subsequent conclusions of what it is not. First, CE cannot guarantee 100-percent effectiveness in finding insider threats before the threat becomes realized. While CE offers opportunities for increased real-time awareness when compared with the current process, it does leverage a subset of—sometimes insufficient—information used today. Furthermore, CE is not immune to insider threats finding ways to operate undetected and below levels that would alert the system. In addition, CE also should not be viewed as an automatic indication of insider threats. The notification indicates the possibility of a potential threat but requires additional analysis to determine the nature of the employee's situation. For example, an individual who misses several credit card payments in a row may alert a CE system of an issue. Further investigation could reveal an unexpected and costly medical emergency in the employee's family.

In contrast with the concerns of civil liberty groups advocating for personal privacy, CE may prove even less invasive than current methods for cleared personnel.

---

[52] Reinvestigations are required to occur *within* specified time periods of five years for Top Secret and ten years for Secret and can occur before the last year in the time period. Additionally, the immense backlog of investigations and reinvestigations means that not everyone undergoes a reinvestigation within the time specified.

As discussed above, CE evaluates the same information used by current investigation and reinvestigation processes, with the difference being the frequency which the data are analyzed. In addition, with CE, employees only receive scrutiny if their data alert the system. Current methods attempting to offer greater awareness of potential insider threats take a random sampling of the population to evaluate at regular intervals, spending time evaluating employees who do not warrant it and associating these evaluations with the individuals; with CE, the data could be anonymized until a trigger is alerted.

Finally, CE will likely not render background investigators obsolete. Instead, CE works with investigators in two ways. First, OPM faces a backlog of more than 500,000 clearance applications.[53] Of these, only approximately 150,000 are for periodic reinvestigations. Even if CE could decrease the backlog by reducing the need for reinvestigating the entire population, OPM still faces hundreds of thousands of applications to be reviewed in addition to the amount of new applications it receives each year. Second, one option for CE is to perform reinvestigations on individuals identified by the monitoring and delaying review for others. The information associated with each case could help OPM prioritize reinvestigations.

What Are Some Challenges to Implementing Continuous Evaluation?

There are several challenges that have prevented the effective synchronization and implementation of CE and insider threat programs. Many of the problems highlighted in the 2014 *Security and Suitability Processes Review Report to the President* remain as of July 2017. Such problems include clarifying and expanding requirements for reporting actions and behavior of employees, along with developing and standardizing performance measures for investigation and adjudication decisions.[54]

First, there are many definitions of CE and insider threat throughout the literature. This has left policymakers and managers in the U.S. government and other industries either to adopt piecemeal definitions or to invent their own. Second, the lack of quantifiable and repeatable data on insiders has required organizations to qualify factors drawn from other disciplines, such as psychology and psychiatry. Bringing in facets of other sciences has helped implementation of pilot testing; however, this remains largely based on theory rather than practice. One major obstacle to gaining primary access to data is that it is highly restricted because of privacy considerations. A second obstacle is that the data are highly sensitive, such as in the case of a company

---

[53]   Data are as of the end of the third quarter in fiscal year 2016 (Clark, 2017).

[54]   The 2014 report also cited a "[a] lack of enterprise Security/Suitability/Credentialing process cost analysis, investment planning for major reform initiatives, and automated records collection capability to enable transition to needed end-to-end automated capabilities" (PAC, 2014).

not wanting to reveal its weaknesses. In addition, developing meaningful case studies for analysis is stymied by the inaccessible nature of actual insiders themselves, who may be in prison or may have fled the country, such as in the cases of Snowden, Manning, and Hasan. A third obstacle is that CE and insider threat pilot programs across all industries are not synchronized. Federal agencies and other industries do not share any information gained during pilot testing processes or the end results of such programs, effectively barring any analysis of comparable results.

Reforms and overcoming these challenges could prove difficult. Interviews with private-sector subject-matter experts led to four important observations related to ongoing CE reform efforts. First, there is an ongoing debate within DoD on whether ownership of the CE problem resides within the Joint Staff Intelligence Directorate or the Joint Staff Operations Directorate, with DoD policymaker-level consensus leaning toward the former.[55] Second, the NISPOM has yet to incorporate violent insider threats and, hence, would not incorporate a case similar to that of Hasan. Third, organizations would need cultural and organizational changes to accept CE and insider threat as part of their strategic missions. Lastly, organizations must balance security clearance, privacy concerns, human resources, and physical and IT security together to create an effective CE program. The greatest challenge to implementing an effective CE and insider threat program, however, may be the ever-changing intentions of insiders themselves.

Findings and Recommendations

Finding 8: The current investigation and adjudication process is time consuming, creating a large backlog of investigations and periodic reinvestigations. There are approximately 416,000 unprocessed security clearance investigations and approximately 156,000 unprocessed periodic reinvestigations. Various disturbances have doubled and tripled the time to process each clearance, which contributes to the backlog of incomplete investigations and adjudications.

Recommendation 8: Prioritize resources and clearance reviews that present the most urgent investigative and adjudicative issues. Incorporating a prioritizing mechanism into CE could reduce the inefficiencies of the clearance review process. The backlog of unprocessed periodic reinvestigations could be significantly diminished; the allocation of resources could be more routinely reevaluated and adjusted to accommodate changes in the volume, variety, and scope of investigations.

Finding 9a: The organization that has had primary security clearance investigating responsibility has faced resource reductions. OPM has experienced

---

[55] Many federal agencies have relied on the Big Sky consulting firm to improve processes related to CE (RAND interviews with government and nongovernment personnel, June 2017).

resource reductions, limiting the office's ability to grow its workforce to address the backlog. OPM estimated the cost of a Tier 3 Secret clearance in 2018 at approximately $430 per person and the cost of a Tier 5 Top Secret clearance at approximately $5,596 per person.

Finding 9b: The cost over the long term for CE might be lower than the cost over the same period using current practices. Current investigations impose rising costs, while CE is estimated to be more cost-efficient in the long term. The greatest costs of the clearance process relate to Top Secret clearances, and this is where the greatest savings occur with CE. Some organizations, such as the State Department, do not even have the data necessary to estimate current costs. While exact costs and savings depend on CE packages selected and population size, estimates revealed that savings might be realized after six years and could be substantial over a longer period.

Recommendation 9: Conduct a detailed cost-benefit analysis to determine projected programmatic costs. Such an analysis should include a detailed comparative breakdown of initial and ongoing costs of the current program and of potential programs that include various aspects of CE. The creation of the National Background Investigations Bureau by EO 13467 has brought significant improvements to the current security clearance process; however, additional steps could be taken to ensure continued efforts at identifying and reducing costs of the investigative and adjudicative process. An overall assessment of the current security clearance process that looks for areas where CE would accelerate periodic reinvestigations, at no cost to their quality, is necessary. There are likely certain areas, such as aspects of the review process, clearance levels, and types of classified areas, where introducing CE processes would address the most stifling backlogs and costs while ensuring that careful review of critical information remained a central focus of reinvestigations.

Finding 10: Despite concerns over personal privacy, CE may be less invasive for the cleared population than current approaches. The substance of the data CE reviews is not new; only the frequency with which the data are reviewed is. Those individuals receiving greater scrutiny would be limited to those that the CE system had identified as having an issue worthy of further investigation, as opposed to all individuals in the entire cleared population.

Recommendation 10: Articulate what CE is and is not. Such a plan should emphasize that while the process of CE is new, the substance is not, and so if it is executed properly, it is no more invasive method than current processes.

Recommendation 11 (overarching): Connect all insider threat information (e.g., security, general counsel, human resources, chief information officer, and other related efforts) to counter insider threats. Fully implement security clearance reciprocity and suitability/fitness reciprocity among U.S. government departments and agencies and merge the security clearance and suitability/fitness programs and processes to improve coordination and gain maximum vetting value from collected data across programs, departments, and agencies. This would limit the greatest benefit from

PII to those involved with CE programs. Those who implement CE programs should have concrete examples of whether additional PII data would bolster insider detection. Available data on previous cases of insider threats should be shared with all those who would benefit. Another aspect of this reciprocity should focus on a better explanation of CE efforts holistically; stakeholders would benefit from a greater understanding that CE intends to remain within the same investigative scope and would only increase the frequency with which individuals are screened. However, this recommendation represents an ideal for information-sharing to produce more effective CE processes. This study did not consider the broader organizational implications of this recommendation, which would require additional research.

Conclusions

Many CE programs, particularly within the government, remain in the early phases and are not yet fully operational. The effectiveness of these programs remains obscure because most results are not yet publicly available, and it could take time to realize measurable benefits and assess success. The efficiency of CE compared with current methods, however, likely indicates a less costly alternative in the long run, especially regarding individuals needing and maintaining a Top Secret clearance. This does not imply that CE presents a flawless solution to all insider threat problems, as novel issues will likely accompany CE. Privacy concerns, the security of data, alternate potential uses of CE information, and issues that have not yet been considered will have to be explored. Furthermore, CE is not a complete replacement of the current system but could serve to improve it. As discussed throughout this report and highlighted in this chapter, many challenges lie ahead in developing CE as a solution to insider threats.

CHAPTER SIX

Conclusion

An often-heard cliché in the U.S. national security, homeland security, and intelligence fields is that our adversary needs to be successful only once, whereas U.S. national security professionals need to be correct every time. The same holds true for preventing harm from the inside. A single trusted insider can do considerable damage; therefore, the process of evaluating personnel must strive to be right every time.

The threat from insiders over the years has been realized. The United States and those under its employ are at grave risk from these threats. There is currently no agreement among the federal government; the IT, cyber, and business communities; and academia on the definition of *insider threat*. There are, however, some shared ideas, interests, and concerns. U.S. department and agency data are at risk but may benefit by considering the physical security of personnel employed by the United States and those who conduct business or visit U.S. facilities. The implementation of CE in security clearance and suitability/fitness programs and processes should be continued. This should include exploring ongoing and additional CE processes to allow for continued improvement relative to insider threat programs. The loss of even a single life is tragic. The actual costs of the loss of classified information and other sensitive data are enormous, as are the increased costs associated with protecting those data. The costs due to the erosion of confidence by U.S. employees, the U.S. population, and our allies are also extremely significant.

The threat is not going away, and, in fact, it is likely increasing. There will almost certainly be more attacks by insiders in the future, causing harm to both U.S. data and employees. The U.S. government must accept this fact and improve vetting to mitigate the threat to the extent possible. CE will likely improve vetting of the trusted workforce in many ways. CE may be an efficient and effective way of providing improved vetting of the U.S. government and contractor workforce.

The problem of defining insider threats and CE will likely continue to evolve. It presents one of the major challenges in current security clearance processes, and its resolution will significantly underwrite improvements in identifying, detecting, monitoring, and responding to both present and future insider threats. Categorizing insiders by intent would mark a critical effort to expand the definition of *insider threat* and focus government visibility on insiders in response to recent disclosures of classified information, acts of physical violence, and espionage. There are potential fiscal benefits and risk reductions by combining the processes for granting security clearances for national security positions and determining suitability for positions in federal law enforcement and other areas of the federal government. CE could improve insider threat programs in both the public and private sectors by making them more efficient, cost-effective, and consistent. Instituting a CE program is not without challenges, including initial implementation challenges. Additional challenges include issues related to privacy—e.g., human resources, IT, and security. The authors of this report acknowledge that more work remains on evaluating this issue but suggest that the potential benefits of CE could outweigh the costs in terms of program budgeting, efficiency, and effectiveness.

References

Air Force Instruction 16-1402, "Operations Support Insider Threat Program Management," August 5, 2014. As of June 19, 2017:
https://fas.org/irp/doddir/usaf/afi16-1402.pdf

Band, Stephen R., Dawn M. Cappelli, Lynn F. Fischer, Andrew P. Moore, Eric D. Shaw, and Randall F. Trzeciak, *Comparing Insider IT Sabotage and Espionage: A Model-Based Analysis*, Pittsburgh, Pa.: Software Engineering Institute, Carnegie Mellon University, CMU/SEI-2006-TR-026, December 2006. As of July 8, 2019:
https://resources.sei.cmu.edu/asset_files/TechnicalReport/2006_005_001_14798.pdf

Berman, Mark, "Chelsea Manning on Leaking Information: 'I Have a Responsibility to the Public,'" *Washington Post*, June 9, 2017. As of September 14, 2017:
https://www.washingtonpost.com/news/post-nation/wp/2017/06/09/chelsea-manning-on-leaking-information-i-have-a-responsibility-to-the-public/?utm_term=.0e734f2e526e

Bishop, Matt, Sophie Engle, Deborah A. Frincke, Carrie Gates, Frank L. Greitzer, Sean Peisert, and Sean Whalen, "A Risk Management Approach to the 'Insider Threat,'" in Christian W. Probst, Jeffrey Hunker, Dieter Gollmann, and Matt Bishop, eds., *Insider Threats in Cyber Security*, Boston, Mass.: Springer, 2010, pp. 115–137.

Booz Allen Hamilton, "The Accidental Insider Threat: Is Your Organization Ready?" panel discussion, September 25, 2012.

Boyd, Aaron, "Manning/Snowden Leaks: The Threat from Within Emerges," *Federal Times*, December 4, 2015.

Capra, Tony, "Snowden Leaks Could Cost Military Billions: Pentagon," NBC News, March 6, 2017. As of September 11, 2017:
https://www.nbcnews.com/news/investigations/snowden-leaks-could-cost-military-billions-pentagon-n46426

Caputo, Deanna D., Greg Stephens, Brad Stephenson, and Minna Kim, "Human Behavior, Insider Threat, and Awareness: An Empirical Study of Insider Threat Behavior," Bedford, Mass.: MITRE Corporation, technical paper, February 2010. As of July 8, 2019:
https://www.mitre.org/publications/technical-papers/human-behavior-insider-threat-and-awareness-an-empirical-study-of-insider-threat-behavior

Caputo, Deanna D., and Gregory D. Stephens, "Detecting Insider Theft of Trade Secrets," Bedford, Mass.: MITRE Corporation, November/December 2009.

Carnegie Mellon University Software Engineering Institute, "Insider Threat," 2017. As of May 23, 2017:
http://www.cert.org/insider-threat/

CERT, "About Us," undated. As of May 23, 2017:
http://www.cert.org/about/

CERT Insider Threat Center, *Common Sense Guide to Mitigating Insider Threats, Fifth Edition*, Pittsburgh, Pa.: Carnegie Mellon University Software Engineering Institute, CMU/SEI-2015-TR-010, December 2016. As of July 8, 2019:
http://resources.sei.cmu.edu/asset_files/TechnicalReport/2016_005_001_484758.pdf

CERT Insider Threat Team, "Unintentional Insider Threats: A Foundational Study," Pittsburgh, Pa.: Carnegie Mellon University Software Engineering Institute, technical report, 2013.

Charney, D. L., "True Psychology of the Insider Spy," *Intelligencer: Journal of the U.S. Intelligence Studies*, Vol. 18, No. 1, 2010, pp. 47–54.

Chesbro, Michael, *Introduction to Insider Threat: A Summary of Information from Multiple Sources*, Washington, D.C.: U.S. Department of Defense, April 20, 2013.

Cisco, "Data Leakage Worldwide: The High Cost of Insider Threats," white paper, San Jose, Calif., March 12, 2014. As of July 8, 2019:
https://www.cisco.com/c/en/us/solutions/collateral/enterprise-networks/data-loss-prevention/white_paper_c11-506224.html

Clark, Charles S., "Government Warms to Continuous Monitoring of Personnel with Clearances," *Defense One*, July 10, 2017. As of August 28, 2017:
http://www.defenseone.com/technology/2017/07/government-warms-continuous-monitoring-personnel-clearances/139314/?oref=d-channelriver

Claycomb, William R., Carly L. Huth, Lori Flynn, David M. McIntire, and Todd B. Lewellen, "Chronological Examination of Insider Threat Sabotage: Preliminary Observations," *Journal of Wireless Mobile Networks, Ubiquitous Computing, and Dependable Applications*, Vol. 3, No. 4, December 2012, pp. 4–20.

Claycomb, William R., and Alex Nicoll, "Insider Threats to Cloud Computing: Directions for New Research Challenges," *2012 IEEE 36th Annual Computer Software and Applications Conference*, IEEE, July 2012.

Connolly, Katie, "Has Release of Wikileaks Documents Cost Lives?" BBC News, December 1, 2010. As of June 20, 2019:
https://www.bbc.com/news/world-us-canada-11882092

Costa, Daniel, "CERT Definition of 'Insider Threat'—Updated," *Insider Threat Blog*, Carnegie Mellon University Software Engineering Institute, March 7, 2017. As of December 3, 2018:
https://insights.sei.cmu.edu/insider-threat/2017/03/cert-definition-of-insider-threat---updated.html

Cummings, Adam, Todd Lewellen, David McIntire, Andrew P. Moore, and Randall F. Trzeciak, *Insider Threat Study: Illicit Cyber Activity Involving Fraud in the U.S. Financial Services Sector*, Pittsburgh, Pa.: Carnegie Mellon University Software Engineering Institute, CMU/SEI-2012-SR-004, July 2012. As of July 8, 2019:
https://resources.sei.cmu.edu/library/asset-view.cfm?assetid=27971

Cyber Security & Information Systems Information Analysis Center, "Insider Threat Workshop," July 2013.

Cybersecurity and Infrastructure Security Agency, "Security Tip (ST04-002): Choosing and Protecting Passwords," last revised November 21, 2018. As of July 9, 2019:
https://www.us-cert.gov/ncas/tips/ST04-002

Dalal, Reeshad Sam, "A Meta-Analysis of the Relationship Between Organizational Citizenship Behavior and Counterproductive Work Behavior," *Journal of Applied Psychology*, Vol. 90, No. 6, December 2005, pp. 1241–1255.

Defense Advanced Research Projects Agency, "Broad Agency Announcement: Cyber Insider Threat (CINDER) Strategic Technology Office," DARPA-BAA-10-84, August 25, 2010.

Defense Office of Hearings and Appeals, homepage, 2019. As of July 9, 2019:
http://ogc.osd.mil/doha/

Defense Security Service, "DoD Insider Threat Management and Analysis Center," undated-a. As of February 2017:
http://www.dss.mil/about_dss/ditmac.html

Defense Security Service, "Insider Threats," undated-b. As of January 23, 2017:
http://www.dss.mil/documents/ci/Insider-Threats.pdf

Department of Homeland Security, "System of Record Notices," undated. As of July 8, 2019:
https://www.dhs.gov/system-records-notices-sorns

Department of Homeland Security, "Privacy Impact Assessment for the Automated Continuous Evaluation System (ACES) Pilot," April 9, 2007.

Department of Homeland Security, "National Cybersecurity and Communications Integration Center, Combating the Insider Threat," May 2, 2014.

DHS—*See* Department of Homeland Security.

DHS Science and Technology Directorate Cyber Security Division, "Insider Threat," March 3, 2016.

DoD Directive 5240.06, "Counterintelligence Awareness and Reporting (CIAR)," May 17, 2011, Incorporating Change 2, July 21, 2017.

DoD Instruction 5200.02, "DoD Personnel Security Program (PSP)," March 21, 2014, Incorporating Change 1, Effective September 9, 2014.

DoD Memorandum 5200.2-R, "Personnel Security Program," January 1987.

DOHA—*See* Defense Office of Hearings and Appeals.

Ebersole, Kyle, "Continuous Evaluation: Welcoming Government Employees to the World of Mass Surveillance," *George Mason Law Review*, Vol. 23, No. 2, 2016, pp. 445–477.

Ehlinger, Samantha, "Finding Feelings: Intelligence Agency Lines Up New Tool for Rooting Out Insider Threats," FedScoop, February 6, 2017. As of July 8, 2019:
https://www.fedscoop.com/finding-feelings-intelligence-agency-lines-new-tool-rooting-insider-threats/

EO 12968—*See* Executive Order 12968.

EO 13467—*See* Executive Order 13467.

EO 13587—*See* Executive Order 13587.

EO 13764—*See* Executive Order 13764.

Executive Order 12968, "Access to Classified Information," *Federal Register*, Vol. 60, No. 151, August 7, 1995, pp. 40245–40254.

Executive Order 13467, "Reforming Processes Related to Suitability for Government Employment, Fitness for Contractor Employees, and Eligibility for Access to Classified National Security Information," *Federal Register*, Vol. 73, No. 128, July 2, 2008, pp. 38103–38108. As of July 8, 2019:
https://fas.org/irp/offdocs/eo/eo-13467.htm

Executive Order 13587, "Structural Reforms to Improve the Security of Classified Networks and the Responsible Sharing and Safeguarding of Classified Information," October 7, 2011. As of July 8, 2019:
https://obamawhitehouse.archives.gov/the-press-office/2011/10/07/
executive-order-13587-structural-reforms-improve-security-classified-net

Executive Order 13764, "Amending the Civil Service Rules, Executive Order 13488, and Executive Order 13467 to Modernize the Executive Branch-Wide Governance Structure and Processes for Security Clearances, Suitability and Fitness for Employment, and Credentialing, and Related Matters," *Federal Register*, Vol. 82, No. 13, January 23, 2017, pp. 8115–8129. As of July 8, 2019:
https://www.federalregister.gov/documents/2017/01/23/2017-01623/
amending-the-civil-service-rules-executive-order-13488-and-executive-order-13467-to-modernize-the

EY, "Managing Insider Threat: A Holistic Approach to Dealing with Risk from Within," 2016. As of June 19, 2017:
http://www.ey.com/Publication/vwLUAssets/EY-managing-inside-threat/
$FILE/EY-managing-inside-threat.pdf

Fitzgerald, Todd, "The Information Security Auditors Have Arrived, Now What?" in Harold F. Tipton and Micki Krause, eds., *Information Security Management Handbook*, New York: Auerbach Publications, 2009.

"Five Habits of Companies That Catch Insiders," Dark Reading, October 22, 2012. As of July 8, 2019:
http://www.darkreading.com/vulnerabilities---threats/
five-habits-of-companies-that-catch-insiders/d/d-id/1138574

Fox, Suzy, Paul E. Spector, and Don Miles, "Counterproductive Work Behavior (CWB) in Response to Job Stressors and Organizational Justice: Some Mediator and Moderator Tests for Autonomy and Emotions," *Journal of Vocational Behavior*, Vol. 59, No. 3, 2001, pp. 291–309.

Fung, Brian, "5.1 Million Americans Have Security Clearances. That's More Than the Entire Population of Norway," *Washington Post*, March 24, 2014.

GAO—*See* Government Accountability Office.

Gelles, Michael G., "Mitigating the Insider Threat: Building a Secure Workforce," Deloitte, March 2012.

Government Accountability Office, *Insider Threats: DoD Should Strengthen Management and Guidance to Protect Classified Information and Systems*, Washington, D.C., GAO-15-544, June 2015.

Greitzer, Frank L., and Thomas A. Ferryman, "Methods and Metrics for Evaluating Analytic Insider Threat Tools," *Proceedings of the 2013 IEEE Security and Privacy Workshops*, 2013, pp. 90–97.

Greitzer, Frank L., and Deborah A. Frincke, "Combining Traditional Cyber Security Audit Data with Psychosocial Data: Towards Predictive Modeling for Insider Threat Mitigation," in Christian W. Probst, Jeffrey Hunker, Dieter Gollmann, and Matt Bishop, eds., *Insider Threats in Cyber Security*, Boston, Mass.: Springer, 2010, pp. 85–113.

Greitzer, Frank L., Deborah A. Frincke, and Mariah Zabriskie, "Social/Ethical Issues in Predictive Insider Threat Monitoring," in Melissa Jane Dark, ed., *Information Assurance and Security Ethics in Complex Systems: Interdisciplinary Perspectives*, Hershey, Pa.: IGI Global, 2010, pp. 132–161.

Greitzer, Frank L., and Ryan E. Hohimer, "Modeling Human Behavior to Anticipate Insider Attacks," *Journal of Strategic Security*, Vol. 4, No. 2, June 2011, pp. 25–48.

Greitzer, Frank L., Christine Noonan, Lars J. Kangas, and Angela Dalton, *Identifying At-Risk Employees: A Behavioral Model for Predicting Potential Insider Threats*, Richland, Wash.: Pacific Northwest National Laboratory, PNNL-19665, September 30, 2010.

Greitzer, Frank L., Patrick R. Paulson, Lars J. Kangas, Lyndsey R. Franklin, Thomas W. Edgar, and Deborah A. Frincke, *Predictive Modeling for Insider Threat Mitigation*, Richland, Wash.: Pacific Northwest National Laboratory, PNNL-SA-65204, April 2009.

Gruys, Melissa L., and Paul R. Sackett, "Investigating the Dimensionality of Counterproductive Work Behavior," *International Journal of Selection and Assessment*, Vol. 11, No. 1, 2003, pp. 30–42.

Hanley, Michael, Tyler Dean, Will Schroeder, Matt Houy, Randall F. Trzeciak, and Joji Montelibano, *An Analysis of Technical Observations in Insider Theft of Intellectual Property Cases*, Pittsburgh, Pa.: Carnegie Mellon University Software Engineering Institute, CMU/SEI-2011-TN-006, February 2011.

Hanley, Michael, and Joji Montelibano, *Insider Threat Control: Using Centralized Logging to Detect Data Exfiltration Near Insider Termination*, Pittsburgh, Pa.: Carnegie Mellon University Software Engineering Institute, CMU/SEI-2011-TN-024, October 2011.

Henderson, William, "A Brief History of the U.S. Personnel Security Program," ClearanceJobs.com, June 29, 2009. As of August 28, 2017:
https://news.clearancejobs.com/2009/06/29/a-brief-history-of-the-u-s-personnel-security-program/

Herbig, Katherine L., Ray A. Zimmerman, and Callie J. Chandler, *The Evolution of the Automated Continuous Evaluation System (ACES) for Personnel Security*, Seaside, Calif.: Defense Personnel and Security Research Center, Technical Report 13-06, November 2013. As of July 8, 2019:
https://apps.dtic.mil/dtic/tr/fulltext/u2/a626819.pdf

IAEA—*See* International Atomic Energy Agency.

IARPA—*See* Intelligence Advanced Research Projects Activity.

Ilgun, Koral, Richard A. Kemmerer, and Phillip A. Porras, "State Transition Analysis: A Rule-Based Intrusion Detection Approach," *IEEE Transactions on Software Engineering*, Vol. 21, No. 3, 1995, pp. 181–199.

Imperva, *Insiders: The Threat Is Already Within*, Hacker Intelligence Initiative Report, Redwood Shores, Calif., 2016. As of July 8, 2019:
https://www.imperva.com/docs/Imperva_HII_Insider_Threat.pdf

INSA—*See* Intelligence and National Security Alliance.

Intelligence Advanced Research Projects Activity, "Scientific Advances to Continuous Insider Threat Evaluation (SCITE)," undated. As of April 24, 2017:
https://www.iarpa.gov/index.php/research-programs/scite

Intelligence and National Security Alliance, *Leveraging Emerging Technologies in the Security Clearance Process*, March 2014.

Intelligence and National Security Alliance, *Assessing the Mind of the Malicious Insider: Using a Behavioral Model and Data Analytics to Improve Continuous Evaluation*, April 2017.

Intelligence and National Security Alliance Cyber Council, "Insider Threat Task Force," September 2013.

International Atomic Energy Agency, *Preventive and Protective Measures Against Insider Threats Implementing Guide*, Vienna, IAEA Nuclear Security Series No. 8, 2008.

Issa, Darrell, Chairman, Committee on Oversight and Government Reform, "Slipping Through the Cracks: How the D.C. Navy Yard Shooting Exposes Flaws in the Federal Security Clearance Process," Staff Report, Committee on Oversight and Government Reform, U.S. House of Representatives, 113th Congress, February 11, 2014. As of August 28, 2017: http://oversight.house.gov/wp-content/uploads/2014/02/Aaron-Alexis-Report-FINAL.pdf

Javitz, H. S., and A. Valdes, "The SRI IDES Statistical Anomaly Detector," in *Proceedings of the IEEE Symposium on Research in Security and Privacy*, May 1991, pp. 316–376.

Joint Security and Suitability Reform Team, "Security and Suitability Process Reform," December 2008.

Kenber, Billy, "Nidal Hasan Sentenced to Death for Fort Hood Shooting Rampage," *Washington Post*, August 28, 2013. As of September 14, 2017: https://www.washingtonpost.com/world/national-security/ nidal-hasan-sentenced-to-death-for-fort-hood-shooting-rampage/2013/08/28/ aad28de2-0ffa-11e3-bdf6-e4fc677d94a1_story.html?utm_term=.60041bf89b67

Kirkpatrick, Michael, Elisa Bertino, and Frederick Sheldon, "An Architecture for Contextual Insider Threat Detection," white paper, 2009, pp. 1–11.

Eileen Kowalski, Tara Conway, Susan Keverline, Megan Williams, Dawn Cappelli, Bradford Willke, and Andrew Moore, *Insider Threat Study: Illicit Cyber Activity in the Government Sector*, Pittsburgh, Pa.: Carnegie Mellon University Software Engineering Institute, January 2008. As of July 9, 2019: https://apps.dtic.mil/dtic/tr/fulltext/u2/a638652.pdf

Langin, Chet, and Shahram Rahimi, "Soft Computing in Intrusion Detection: The State of the Art," *Journal of Ambient Intelligence and Humanized Computing*, Vol. 1, No. 2, 2010, pp. 133–145.

Langin, Chet, Hongbo Zhou, and Shahram Rahimi, "A Model to Use Denied Internet Traffic to Indirectly Discover Internal Network Security Problems," *Performance, Computing and Communications Conference, 2008*, IEEE International, 2008.

Lenca, P., P. Meyer, B. Vaillant, and S. Lallich, "On Selecting Interestingness Measures for Association Rules: User Oriented Description and Multiple Criteria Decision Aid," *European Journal of Operational Research*, Vol. 184, No. 2, 2008, pp. 610–626.

LexisNexis, "Making Sense of Data: The LexisNexis Data Analytics Supercomputer (DAS) Delivers Results," white paper, undated. As of August 14, 2017: http://www.lexisnexis.com/risk/downloads/whitepaper/das-spotlight.pdf

LexisNexis, "Using Identity Management and Predictive Analytics to Prevent Fraud and Improve Provider and Member Management?" February 6, 2013.

Marine Corps Installations East–Marine Corps Base Camp Lejeune, "What Is Continuous Evaluation?" undated. As of June 19, 2017: https://www.mcieast.marines.mil/Portals/33/Documents/Adjutant/Security%20Manager/ SharePortal%20Documents/Continuous%20Evaluation%20Short%20Take.pdf

Martinez-Moyano, Ignacio J., Eliot H. Rich, Stephen H. Conrad, and David F. Andersen, "Modeling the Emergence of Insider Threat Vulnerabilities," *Proceedings of the 2006 Winter Simulation Conference*, IEEE, 2006, pp. 562–568.

Martinez-Moyano, Ignacio J., Eliot Rich, Stephen Conrad, David F. Andersen, and Thomas R. Stewart, "A Behavioral Theory of Insider-Threat Risks: A System Dynamics Approach," *ACM Transactions on Modeling and Computer Simulation*, Vol. 18, No. 2, Article 7, April 2008.

Maybury, Mark, Penny Chase, Brant Cheikes, Dick Brackney, Sara Matzner, Tom Hetherington, Brad Wood, Conner Sibley, Jack Marin, Tom Longstaff, Lance Spitzner, Jed Haile, John Copeland, and Scott Lewandowski, *Analysis and Detection of Malicious Insiders*, Bedford, Mass.: MITRE Corporation, 2005.

Memmott, Mark, and Eyder Peralta, "Attack at the Navy Yard: Gunman and 12 Victims Killed," NPR, September 16, 2013. As of September 11, 2017:
http://www.npr.org/sections/thetwo-way/2013/09/16/223023740/
developing-shooting-at-u-s-navy-yard-in-washington-d-c

Moore, Andrew P., Dawn M. Cappelli, Thomas C. Caron, Eric Shaw, Derrick Spooner, and Randall F. Trzeciak, *A Preliminary Model of Insider Theft of Intellectual Property*, Pittsburgh, Pa.: Carnegie Mellon University Software Engineering Institute, CMU/SEI-2011-TN-013, June 2011.

Moore, Andrew P., Dawn M. Cappelli, and Randall F. Trzeciak, "The 'Big Picture' of Insider IT Sabotage Across U.S. Critical Infrastructures," in Salvatore J. Stolfo, Steven M. Bellovin, Angelos D. Keromytis, Shlomo Hershkop, Sean W. Smith, and Sara Sinclair, *Insider Attack and Cyber Security: Beyond the Hacker*, Boston, Mass.: Springer, 2008, pp. 17–52.

Moore, Andrew P., Michael Hanley, and David Mundie, *A Pattern for Increased Monitoring for Intellectual Property Theft by Departing Insiders*, Pittsburgh, Pa.: Carnegie Mellon University Software Engineering Institute, CMU/SEI-2012-TR-008, April 2012.

Moore, Andrew P., David Mcintire, David Mundie, and David Zubrow, "The Justification of a Pattern for Detecting Intellectual Property Theft by Departing Insiders," *Proceedings of the 19th Conference on Pattern Languages of Programs*, Hillside Group, 2012.

Muñoz, Carlo, "Brennan: Intel Leaks Have 'Absolutely' Damaged US National Security," *The Hill*, August 11, 2012. As of September 11, 2017:
http://thehill.com/policy/defense/
243179-brennan-intel-leaks-have-absolutely-damaged-us-national-security

National Counterintelligence and Security Center, "Resources: Top Issues: Insider Threat," undated. As of January 23, 2017:
https://www.ncsc.gov/issues/ithreat/

National Insider Threat Task Force, *Clarification of Enterprise Audit Management (EAM), User Activity Monitoring (UAM), Continuous Monitoring, and Continuous Evaluation*, NITTF-2014-008, March 2014.

National Security Institute, *Improving Security from the Inside Out: A Business Case for Corporate Security Awareness*, Medway, Mass., 2004.

National Security Telecommunications and Information Systems Security Advisory Memorandum, "The Insider Threat to U.S. Government Information Systems," INFOSEC/1-99, July 1999.

NCSC—*See* National Counterintelligence and Security Center.

NITTF—*See* National Insider Threat Task Force.

Noonan, Thomas, and Edmund Archuleta, *The National Infrastructure Advisory Council's Final Report and Recommendations on the Insider Threat to Critical Infrastructures*, National Infrastructure Advisory Council, April 8, 2008.

NSTISSAM—*See* National Security Telecommunications and Information Systems Security Advisory Memorandum.

Obama, Barack, "National Insider Threat Policy and Minimum Standards for Executive Branch Insider Threat Programs," presidential memorandum, Washington, D.C., November 21, 2012. As of July 8, 2019:
https://obamawhitehouse.archives.gov/the-press-office/2012/11/21/
presidential-memorandum-national-insider-threat-policy-and-minimum-stand

ODNI—*See* Office of the Director of National Intelligence.

Office of the Director of National Intelligence, "Continuous Evaluation—Overview," undated. As of June 19, 2017:
https://www.dni.gov/index.php/ncsc-how-we-work/ncsc-security-executive-agent/
ncsc-continuous-evaluation-overview

Office of the Director of National Intelligence, "IRTPA Title III Annual Report for 2010," February 15, 2011.

Office of the Director of National Intelligence, *2014 Report on Security Clearance Determinations*, April 2015. As of August 30, 2017:
https://fas.org/sgp/othergov/intel/clear-2014.pdf

Office of Inspector General, *Evaluation of the Department of State's Security Clearance Process*, U.S. Department of State, July 2017. As of August 18, 2017:
https://oig.state.gov/system/files/esp-17-02_report.pdf

Office of the Under Secretary of Defense, "Extension of Periodic Reinvestigation Timelines to Address the Background Investigation Backlog," Washington, D.C., January 17, 2017. As of July 8, 2019:
http://www.cdse.edu/documents/toolkits-psa/extension.pdf

OIG—*See* Office of Inspector General.

OPM—*See* U.S. Office of Personnel Management.

PAC—*See* Performance Accountability Council.

Performance Accountability Council, *Suitability and Security Processes Review Report to the President*, February 2014.

Personnel Security, "Continuous Evaluation," undated. As of July 8, 2019:
http://www.dami.army.pentagon.mil/site/PerSec/PS-ContEval.aspx

Prasad, Sakthi, "U.S. Brings Fraud Charges Against Firm That Vetted Snowden," Reuters, January 23, 2014. As of October 3, 2018:
https://www.reuters.com/article/us-usa-usis/
u-s-brings-fraud-charges-against-firm-that-vetted-snowden-idUSBREA0M0BD20140123

Public Law 108-458, Intelligence Reform and Terrorism Prevention Act of 2004, December 17, 2004.

Randazzo, Marisa Reddy, Michelle Keeney, Eileen Kowalski, Dawn Cappelli, and Andrew Moore, *Insider Threat Study: Illicit Cyber Activity in the Banking and Finance Sector*, Pittsburgh, Pa.: Carnegie Mellon University Software Engineering Institute, CMU/SEI-2004-TR-021, June 2005.

RAND Corporation, "Security Mandatory Annual Refresher Training (SMART) 2016 Security Training Presentation," undated.

Rashid, Fahmida Y., "Learn from Past Incidents," *eWeek*, March 5, 2012. As of July 8, 2019:
http://www.eweek.com/c/a/Security/
Insider-Security-Threats-10-Tactics-to-Stop-These-Data-Breaches-530393

Raytheon, "Best Practices for Mitigating and Investigating Insider Threats," 2009.

Shaw, E. D., and L. F. Fischer, "Ten Tales of Betrayal: The Threat to Corporate Infrastructures by Information Technology Insiders Analysis and Observations," Monterey, Calif.: Defense Personnel Security Research Center, 2005.

Shaw, Eric D., Lynn F. Fischer, and Andrée E. Rose, *Insider Risk Evaluation and Audit*, Monterey, Calif.: Defense Personnel Security Research Center, Technical Report 09-02, August 2009.

Silowash, George, "Building an Insider Threat Program: Five Important Categories of Tools (Part 1 of 2)," *Insider Threat Blog*, Carnegie Mellon University Software Engineering Institute, July 26, 2016. As of July 8, 2019:
https://insights.sei.cmu.edu/insider-threat/2016/07/
insider-threat-program-five-important-classes-tools.html

Silowash, George J., Todd Lewellen, Joshua W. Burns, and Daniel L. Costa, *Detecting and Preventing Data Exfiltration Through Encrypted Web Sessions via Traffic Inspection*, Pittsburgh, Pa.: Carnegie Mellon University Software Engineering Institute, CMU/SEI-2013-TN-012, March 2013.

Silowash, George, Dawn Cappelli, Andrew Moore, Randall Trzeciak, Timothy J. Shimeall, and Lori Flynn, *Common Sense Guide to Mitigating Insider Threats, Fourth Edition*, Pittsburgh, Pa.: Carnegie Mellon University Software Engineering Institute, 2012.

Stewart, Scott, "The Problem with Background Investigations," *Stratfor*, July 4, 2013. As of August 28, 2017:
https://worldview.stratfor.com/weekly/problems-background-investigations#/entry/jsconnect?client_id=644347316&target=%2Fdiscussion%2Fembed%3Fp%3D%252Fdiscussion%252Fembed%252F%26vanilla_identifier%3D236082%26vanilla_url%3Dhttps%253A%252F%252Fworldview.stratfor.com%252Fweekly%252Fproblems-background-investigations%26vanilla_cat

Suciu, Peter, "What Is the Real Impact of the Security Clearance Backlog?" ClearanceJobs.com, March 27, 2017. As of August 28, 2017:
https://news.clearancejobs.com/2017/03/27/real-impact-security-clearance-backlog/

Sutphin, Michelle J., "NISPPAC Security Policy Updates," briefing, National Industrial Security Program Policy Advisory Committee, updated October 9, 2017.

Thomson Reuters Special Services, "Insider Threat," undated. As of July 9, 2019:
https://www.trssllc.com/insider-threat/

TransUnion, "Threat Monitoring Solutions: Using Changes in Behavior as Leading Indicators of Threats," 2016. As of August 14, 2017:
https://www.transunion.com/resources/transunion/doc/solutions/resources/
solution-gov-threat-monitoring-solutions-as.pdf

TRSS—*See* Thomson Reuters Special Services.

U.S. Department of Defense, Defense Security Service, Counterintelligence Directorate, "Insider Threats: Combating the Enemy Within Your Organization," brochure, undated.

U.S. Department of Defense, *National Industrial Security Program Operating Manual*, DoD 5220.22-M, February 2006, Incorporating Change 2, May 18, 2016. As of July 9, 2019:
http://www.esd.whs.mil/Portals/54/Documents/DD/issuances/dodm/522022M.pdf

U.S. Department of Justice, DOJ Order 0901, "Insider Threat," approved on February 12, 2014.

U.S. Office of Personnel Management, *Agency Financial Report: Fiscal Year 2016*, November 2016. As of August 28, 2017:
https://www.opm.gov/about-us/budget-performance/performance/2016-agency-financial-report.pdf

U.S. Office of Personnel Management, "Statement of Kathleen McGettigan, Acting Director, U.S. Office of Personnel Management, Before the Committee on Oversight and Government Reform, United States House of Representatives, on Improving Security and Efficiency at OPM and the National Background Investigations Bureau," February 2, 2017.

Viebeck, Elise, and Cleve R. Wootson Jr., "Fort Lauderdale Suspect Claimed Government Was Controlling His Mind Months Before Shooting," *Washington Post*, January 8, 2017. As of September 14, 2017:
https://www.washingtonpost.com/news/post-nation/wp/2017/01/08/fort-lauderdale-shooting-suspect-claimed-government-was-controlling-his-mind-months-before-shooting/?utm_term=.39dffeb1f221

Wood, B., "An Insider Threat Model for Adversary Simulation," in *Proceedings of the Research on Mitigating the Insider Threat on Information Systems, August 30–September 1*, No. 2, Arlington, Va., 2000.